World
Catholicism Today

Translated by
EDMOND BONIN

World
Catholicism
Today

by Joseph Folliet

The Newman Press · 1961 · Westminster, Maryland

This is a translation of *Le catholicisme mondial aujourd'hui,* number 54 in the series *"Rencontres"* published by Les Editions du Cerf, Paris.

Nihil obstat: EDWARD A. CERNY, s.s., s.t.d.
    Censor Librorum

Imprimatur: FRANCIS P. KEOUGH, d.d.
    Archbishop of Baltimore
    January 3, 1961

Library of Congress Catalog Card Number: 61-8968
Printed in the United States of America

Contents

World
Catholicism Today

chapter one

A Century
of
Church History

Two stage productions dazzled Paris in 1858. *Le fils naturel,* a typical *roman à thèse* by Alexandre Dumas *fils,* tried to twist morality to particular ends; and Offenbach's *Orphée aux enfers* carried away the Emperor's festivities with its giddy pace.

Three other events that year stirred intellectual circles far more deeply. Pierre-Joseph Proudhon published his most important work, *De la Justice dans la Révolution et dans l'Eglise,* in which, with a strange blend of well-nursed fury and unconscious nostalgia, he acquitted himself of his debt toward God and those who represent Him on earth. In Rome, the Academy of Saint Thomas was founded under the patronage of the medieval thinker whom it had become the fashion for philosophers and scholars to quote. In Lourdes, a tiny village in the Pyrenees, the shepherdess Bernadette saw the Immaculate Conception.

3

If time can be divided into periods at all, such happenings make that year a significant starting-point for a comparison between the beginning and the end of the century extending from 1858 to 1958.

*

In 1858 the Catholic Church was barely beginning to recover from the wounds dealt her by the French Revolution and still had to combat the effects of it in just about every quarter, starting with Italy, where the *Risorgimento* and the House of Savoy threatened the independence of the papal city of Rome.

We of the twentieth century but ill appreciate the ravages wrought by the Revolution, not only in France but in the whole of Europe and, as a result, in the entire world. Without over-dramatizing the plight of Catholicism in the first half of the nineteenth century, we must, to appraise it correctly, visualize cities and even country districts teeming with dechristianized crowds, especially among the younger members of the working classes. The bourgeois elite regarded the Church with feelings ranging from hostility and defiance to scepticism and polite caution. So-called liberal governments persecuted the Faith more or less overtly, and conservative states sometimes used it for selfish ends. Frightful intellectual regress followed when theological institutes were in-

4

hibited or closed and religious orders suppressed. The clergy were not numerous enough, and too many of them were either old and ineffective or young and poorly trained. Countless charitable organizations disappeared entirely, and foreign missions received little or no support.

To measure the decline in the quality of theological speculation, it suffices to compare the works of *abbé* Grégoire with those of the "new theologians," Maistre or Lamennais. Grégoire may have been a Gallican and somewhat of a demagogue, but he was intellectually honest and well trained. Though hardly reliable, he was more reliable than they; in a word, he was a true theologian. To plumb the depths of that age's dechristianization, we have only to reread Alfred de Musset's *Confession d'un enfant du siècle* and the memoirs of Lacordaire or Gratry. So rarely did the men of Paris attend religious services that they completely forgot proper church etiquette—and this to such an extent that, when they first flocked to Notre-Dame to relish Lacordaire's romantically fervent oratory, they neglected to doff their hats and quite unself-consciously kept on smoking. In many a *lycée* opened under the Restoration and directed by ecclesiastical provosts, it was not uncommon for collegians to march up to the altar rail, receive communion and keep the consecrated hosts to seal their letters with.

Earthquakes loosen ageless oaks and force them to shoot out new roots or die. So did the Revolution constrain the Church to break with the past, to reassess and modernize herself at the cost of intense pain and heavy losses.

According to the temper of the time, many looked upon the Church as an anachronism, an innocuous curiosity left over from days long past. Even those bound to her by a sentimental attachment felt estranged from her by intellectual considerations. Thus could Jouffroy write his famous *Comment finissent les dogmes;* thus could the young romanticists—like Hugo, Sainte-Beuve and Guérin—follow Lamennais into apostasy. Philosophers—whether deists like Victor Cousin, pantheists like the post-Kantian Three in Germany, positivists like Auguste Comte, socialists like Proudhon and Marx or nationalists like Mazzini —strained to see who could ring loudest the death knell of Catholic beliefs and institutions. Though the revolutionists thought they had buried the last pope in the person of Pius VI, the nineteenth-century novelist Ponson du Terrail accused them not so much of making an empty boast as of anticipating the victory his own generation was to win. In proposing a treaty with the Superior General of the Jesuits, Auguste Comte himself was motivated, not by intellectual sympathy, but by political realism.

6

After the July monarchy, the ideology of liberalism rode on triumphantly, conquering nation upon nation and compelling even the absolute states of Russia and Austria to reconsider their position. It contaminated the thinking of many Catholics who hankered for freedom. For the majority of unbelieving liberals the Church was a time-worn obstacle which they needed not bother pushing aside since she would soon fall of herself. The condemnation of liberalism by religious authorities, and especially by Popes Gregory XVI and Pius IX, was well founded and justified. We know that today; but at the time it only convinced the liberals that they were right and led them to despise the Church all the more for refusing to accept modern ideas and "progress."

As we can see from Victor Hugo's invective against "Pope Mastaï" after the Napoleonic *coup d'état,* the ideas and aspirations of intellectuals and statesmen were echoed in literature and in the press. Indeed, that bright new sword—the daily newspaper—was deadly in the hands of the liberal *bourgeoisie. Les Débats, Le Siècle,* the official organ of anticlericalism, and other important newspapers throughout France proved that the liberal bourgeois were in control and demonstrated the power they wielded over public opinion in nascent democracies. It was a time when ideas carried the day—ideas handed down ready-made by the almighty press. Yet it seems that the Church had not sized up this "fourth power," as evinced by an eminent cardinal's quip to the effect that Catholic journalists should be used to reclaim the Pontine Marshes.

Every school of thought and almost every source of power merged into a single movement. Indefinite though it was, this organization—loosely called Freemasonry—was most articulate and, at least among the Latins, became openly anti-Church. The economists of the day contrasted the prosperity of Protestant countries with the poverty and stagnation of Catholic ones. The profound Catalan philosopher Balmès devoted much thought to the problem, so serious did it seem. But for the most part, the economists who vaunted England's opulence jumped to conclusions without having ascertained exactly what religion had to do with it as against coal, for example, in that age of the steam engine.

Weakened from without, Catholicism was also suffering within. Again the trouble was liberalism. Although many of the resulting disputes were only the cavil of individuals or small groups who agreed on essentials but stayed aloof for reasons of petty politics, these exhausting attacks diverted the attention and energy of polemicists and prevented men like Dupanloup and Veuillot from studying grave social problems. While Catholics were busy elsewhere, a whole new industrial world sprang up; the working classes took shape while there was no one around to understand their nature or their needs—no one, that is, but a few farseeing men like Frédéric Ozanam, Antoine Chevrier and Don Bosco.

The thorny and seemingly insoluble problem of Rome and the papal states also absorbed much thought and effort, and for a long time practically paralyzed Catholicism in Italy. To most, the popes' spiritual independence appeared inseparable from their temporal power. According to La Guéronnière, no one had analyzed the situation so perceptively as Napoleon III, but the imperial dreamer lacked the persuasiveness and the power to impose his views on others. Moreover, the mentality of the day made difficult of acceptance any reasonable solution like the Lateran Treaty later signed by Pius XI.

Occasionally there shone a ray of hope. With his newspaper, *L'Avenir,* Lamennais spoke to the heart of France and Europe and even Latin America; but when he defected from the Faith and was condemned by Rome, his golden dreams tarnished. Backed by the Church and especially the Archbishop of Paris, the efforts of Frédéric Ozanam seemed assured of success but were reduced to nought by the crisis of 1848 and the Prince-President's *coup d'état.*

Far from being moribund, however, Catholicism was inspiring many vital works at that time and promising more for the future. With Ozanam and Pauline-Marie Jaricot, the Society of Saint Vincent de Paul and the Propagation of the Faith marched triumphantly around the world; humbly and quietly, Armand de Melun and Sister Rosalie fostered the Catholic Social Movement; Archbishop de Ségur organized numerous good works; and Taparelli d'Azeglio, that lofty and solitary thinker, rediscovered the natural law. The Faith was active in Belgium; militant in Ireland under O'Connell; awakening, fresh and energetic in the young democracy that was the United States; tenacious in Canada, where the British failed to convert French-speaking Catholics to Protestantism; and progressing slowly but surely in Germany, with Joseph Görres in the realm of speculation, and Kolping and Ketteler in the field of social practice. A convert from Judaism, Venerable Libermann gave new life to the foreign missions by reactivating the Fathers of the Holy Ghost; to the same end Bishop de Mazenod founded the Oblates of Mary Immaculate; Marion-Brésillac, the *Missions africaines;* and Cardinal Lavigerie, the White Fathers. That period witnessed many saints and many kinds of holiness, from that of the *curé* d'Ars or Antoine Chevrier to that of Don Bosco or Joseph-Benedict Cottolengo. Then there was the inspiring figure of John

Henry Cardinal Newman, which dominated England and all Christendom.

But, on the whole, the season was richer in buds than in fruit, fuller of promise than of achievement. As proof, let us consider Pius IX, who became a prisoner in the Vatican after the defeat of his army. Never was a pope more tenderly loved and more fiercely hated, more warmly praised and more foully vilified. With painful and sometimes bitter lucidity, he unflaggingly battled the evils of the day and declared that his successor would have a mammoth task to perform. But, as a matter of fact, his successor, Leo XIII, reaped the fruit of Pius' hard sowing: from the same furrows as the *Quanta cura* and the *Syllabus,* those bugbears of the liberals, there sprang up the encyclicals *Immortale Dei,* on the Christian organization of states, and *Rerum novarum,* on the condition of the working classes.

*

Add a hundred years, and how different everything is! Some had taken Bossuet's words concerning the Duchess of Orléans and applied them to the Church, announcing, "She is ill, she is dying, she is dead." They were ready to bury her in oblivion with a funeral march on themes from *The Twilight of the Gods*—and, lo! she is more vibrantly alive, more active than ever before. Pharmacist Homais, the prophet of the new era of

11

progress, lies in a little Norman cemetery between the Bovary family vault and the grave of *curé* Bournisien while another priest is still saying Mass in a nearby church and Homais' descendants are following Father Loew's Lenten course on television. So it ever is with all the Homais throughout the world—and there were plenty of them in the last century.

Just as that century was not incurably ill, neither is this one perfectly well. The Church lives but bears the scars of old wounds, and each new day deals her another blow. Consider, for instance, the Church of Silence in the Iron Curtain countries; the many millions of pagans yet to be converted; the huge dechristianized segments of countries that were once Catholic; the demoralized hordes; the intellectual or spiritual crises brought on by the profound changes our civilization is undergoing; the missionary problems indirectly created by the emancipation of colonies; and the spinelessness, the frailty and—worst of all—the mediocrity of countless self-satisfied and routine Catholics.

Still, what an encouraging glow on the Church's cheek! The old ideologies—liberalism, socialism and nationalism—have exhausted themselves along with their potentialities for good or evil, yet Catholic doctrine remains strong, intact, eternal and actual, timeless and timely. Because of the Catholic

Social Movement, the Church has made her teaching on sociology broader, more precise, more concrete. Her philosophy of war and peace answers the needs and calms the fears of today's world, and the whole universe hearkens to the popes' messages broadcast and printed by media of which Catholics may well be proud.

Small wonder, then, that there are so many converts among the intellectuals, the scholars, the artists, the writers and the technical experts; small wonder that students are beginning to fill college chapels; small wonder that, throughout the world and even in non-Christian countries, peoples and their leaders are turning toward the Church and specifically toward the popes, who, as it were, personify her.

In the last century very few politicians and statesmen dared profess their faith openly, and those who did—Daniel O'Connell, Garcia Moreno and Montalembert, for example—were thrust into the limelight. Nowadays many political leaders, in non-communist nations, quietly and unobtrusively proclaim their adherence to Catholicism. Pagan India has even sought the services of a Catholic— and a Jesuit, no less—Father D'Souza. We may fear that all this is too good to be true and feel apprehensive lest parties and governments compromise the very Catholics whose support they so eagerly seek.

Elsewhere, a vast wave of mission-mindedness has carried priests and laymen to the shores of new nations; and, here and there, as in Uganda and Cameroun, the Spirit has breathed a whirlwind. In the midst of race conflicts, whether in Africa or in the United States, the Church stands as the impartial arbitrator who lovingly and fearlessly defends the rights of man.

Something akin to that missionary movement is sweeping over lands which have long been Catholic. Whether spontaneous or suggested by Rome, the modernizing of nuns' costumes is symbolic of inner renewal: from museum pieces, they are becoming the practical garments of doers of the word. The same spirit is reshaping parish life and activities to fit present-day needs. It is vivifying widespread charitable organizations, such as *Le Secours catholique* in France, *Caritas* in Germany and the National Catholic Welfare Conference in the United States; and amazingly varied apostolic movements, such as Catholic Action, the Young Catholic Workers, the Legion of Mary and the *Pro civitate christiana*, that body of apostles founded by Don Rossi in the kindly tradition of the *poverello* of Assisi.

Since these points will be developed in the course of the book, there is no need to labor them now. Instead, I shall conclude this chapter with a synopsis of a telling event that is particularly rich in symbolism.

In 1858, in an out-of-the-way region in the Pyrenees, a little shepherdess with big eyes saw a lovely lady in white who declared, "I am the Immaculate Conception." The "enlightened" newspapers of the time derided the whole episode; the police stepped in and forbade God to work miracles; religious authorities long maintained a prudent reserve. And now, a hundred years later, by every known means of transportation, from every point on the globe, "out of every tribe, every language, every people, every nation," crowds pour into Lourdes. They kneel and pray and sing hymns before the grotto where the shepherd girl beheld her vision. The French government counts on this steady flow of pilgrims with their emblems to improve the financial condition of the Fourth Republic; and yet, the Post Office Department, though it is the laughingstock of all France, remains too stubbornly anticlerical to issue a commemorative stamp.

The Lord has ways which disconcert the wisdom of the over-wise and the prudence of the over-prudent. The antitheses that mark the period which extends from 1858 to 1958 and spans the second half of the last century and the first half of this one forcefully assert the power of the spirit and the vitality of the Church.

15

chapter two

A Geography
of
Contemporary Catholicism

I had just flown from Vancouver to Chicago. Naturally, I was a bit apprehensive about my first contact with this large American city, this hideous and lovable metropolis of the Midwest. No sooner had the plane landed than I was met by two priests, one a Belgian and the other a Frenchman, both studying at the University of Chicago—that curious institution where, according to malicious gossip, Jewish professors expound Thomism to materialistic students.

My two escorts led me to Crossroads, a home for girl students from all over the world. Among the young laywomen who operated it and greeted me like a brother, I saw Belgians, Frenchwomen, Americans, Chinese, Indians and Vietnamese. Despite the variety of races, we experienced no shyness, no uneasiness. I recognized an old friend, Doctor Zacharias, who, though born in Germany and later made a British subject, had worked in the Malay Archipelago, India and China, and had come to spend his last years in the United States near his Chinese friend, Cardinal Tien. We all sang and prayed together—in Latin, the universal language. I felt at home.

The next day, we visited the Back of the Yard, an unusual committee headed by an Irish-American and dedicated to solving local problems. We chatted like brothers, and again I felt at home. From there we went to one of Baroness de Hueck's Friendship Houses, which sheltered all sorts of white people and all shades of colored. Once more, far from being uncomfortable, I felt at home. One evening I attended a function at a nearby parish, and neither the priests nor the parishioners were strangers to me. I felt at home.

That is one of the miracles of Catholicism: that extraordinary unity whereby a real Catholic, as soon as he meets another real Catholic, is at home wherever he may be. As Hilaire Belloc put it, there is everywhere the same faith, the same worship, the same language and the same good wine—at least in the form of Mass wine.

Many outsiders are aware of Catholic unity but tend to think of it as uniformity. They are mistaken. Long ago the Schoolmen defined beauty as "unity amid variety." The unity of the Church includes an astonishing variety which disconcerts

18

those few non-members—especially Protestants—
who can perceive it.

Much of this diversity is due to geography and
is conditioned by soil, climate and culture. Awkward as they may be, expressions like "the Church
of France" and "French Catholicism" are accurate,
for there is a specifically French way of being a
Catholic, just as there are specifically German and
Chilean and Brazilian and Chinese ways. As the
kingdom of Christ is established in new lands, this
multiformity increases and yields almost infinite
nuances which progressively enrich the treasury of
the Church.

In the present chapter I should like to outline a
geography of contemporary Catholicism, "a geography of the heart of Catholicism," as Georges
Duhamel has said. I should also like to demonstrate that the Church's plantings throw out roots,
and that the very soil which is thus worked on and
worked in nourishes with its own substance any
such embodiment of the spirit. The lesson learned
may be useful, since we Frenchmen tend to judge
and settle world problems in the light of conditions existing at home.

*

Anyone who glances at a religious map of the
world will soon notice that, geopolitically, twenti-

19

eth-century Catholicism can boast of groupings of local Churches spread throughout vast areas which share similar conditions and characteristics. Such an impression is neither quite false nor quite true. After all, every generality admits of exceptions, and regions differ among themselves all the way from nuance to opposition. Moreover, any such analysis would remain static and furnish a cutaway illustration rather than a graph of Catholicism. The fact is that, since history and the spirit work everywhere, we must carefully search today's accomplishments for tomorrow's potentialities.

*

Charity and reverence both urge us to give first place to the Church of Silence. Spread over immense sections of the globe and very densely populated, she is kept in a sort of catacomb existence by the violent or insidious persecutions and the totalitarian tyranny of atheistic communism. We know something of what goes on in this one-track ideological empire; but our knowledge is general, and the information we gather about particular countries may, for some, be fairly detailed and accurate and up-to-date, but, for others, quite fragmentary and vague and stale. However, despite the news which eventually filters through to us, we learn nothing of the daily life of these Catholics and, having never experienced anything similar, we find it difficult to understand what we hear about them. We Christians in the free world protest against the persecutions suffered by our brethren in communist lands; but, because so few of us can imagine the daily plight of these victims, our representations often sound abstract and conventional.

There are signs, nevertheless, which we must heed. We know that, in spite of occasional lulls, the persecution in China rages on; we know that Chinese Catholics are being denounced, calumniated, tracked down and banished, often imprisoned and sometimes martyred; but we also know that, except for inevitable defections and betrayals, they are resisting communism admirably. The last words of Father Tang—among the most noble ever spoken by a Christian—testify to those three realities: persecution, the soul's resistance and martyrdom. In the foulest tradition of the tsars, Russian imperialism has practically wiped out the "Uniates," those Catholics who are united with Rome and yet use the Slavic language and liturgy; in the Baltic states, bishops and priests have been decimated or deported as ruthlessly as their flocks. The fate of our Hungarian brethren has been summed up in the inhuman treatment inflicted on Cardinal Mindszenty; that of our Czechoslovakian brethren, in the enforced seclusion of Archbishop Beran. Communist satellites have rejected the Marxist theory that a change in the state's economic structure suffices to eradicate religion. Aware that violence cannot suppress Catholicism overnight, they are now trying to tame the forces of religion and make

21

them a household pet by practicing a vexatious neo-Josephism and establishing national Churches. Although Yugoslavia keeps asserting her independence of the Kremlin, let us not be deceived as to the freedom of the Church in that small "Titotalitarian" world.

Humanly speaking, now, must we despair and count only on a miracle? Or wait for World War III and the atom bomb, and then start over from scratch? God forbid! Common sense should remind us that Marxism holds no eternal promise; bolshevism, even less; Stalinism died with its founder, and Khrushchevism will follow sooner or later. Over and above that, our Christian sense teaches us that the Church is immortal.

A glimmer of hope appears here and there in the dark night. Poland has regained a kind of half-freedom and may be a sign of things to come. What is happening in that crucified country (which the romantics used to call "the Christ of nations") has more than national significance: whether the outcome be failure or success, it will have repercussions in the entire world. Poland today is a crucible, a test and a hope. Her religious leader, the great Cardinal Wyszinski, has shown that he is fully aware of his responsibilities.

Persecuted almost continually since 1933 by nazis and later by communists, the Catholics of

Eastern Germany have been so purified and strengthened that they appreciate the difference between the spiritual and the temporal. They refuse to let their faith be politicized; instead, they risk everything for it, accepting lowliness, poverty and silence to insure its purity. Sometimes their scale of values prompts them to pass harsh judgments on Western Germany, so snugly ensconced in the easy chair of economic prosperity.

A recent happening allows us to surmise the condition of Catholics in a satellite country. Condemned to labor in the mines, various priests and religious sought out and fraternized with workers who had been led astray by communist promises. As friendship grew, the lost sheep realized that only the message of Christ would not deceive them. They examined their conscience and repudiated the errors, deeds and omissions of Christians who had contributed to the success of the lay religion called communism.

In Red China, Catholics are heroically clinging to their faith through the long-drawn-out persecution, while missionaries are working in other Chinese communities in the non-communist world. Soon, perhaps, both halves of that Church will come together again.

Groundless optimism would be wrong, but so would despair. After the revolution of the bour-

geois and the liberals, came a second revolution—
that of the socialists—followed by a wave of broken
promises; and now a third is brewing, heralded by
the deeds done in Warsaw and Budapest. By en-
joining detachment and inspiring meditation, persecution itself (as observed in Poland) stimulates
the faithful in the Church of Silence to take their
rightful place at this stage of the human race's
progress toward God.

*

At the opposite pole from the Church of Silence
—if not geographically, at least psychologically and
politically—stands a community which, for lack of
a better name, I shall call Irish-Anglo-Saxon. Its
unity rests on its common use of the English
language as well as on concepts disseminated in
that language, especially "the American way of
life." Persecuted by Protestant majorities not too
long ago, the Catholicism of this group retains a
few traits developed under stress: it possesses a
militant, conquering spirit; and, while reacting
against some aspects of Protestantism, it has more
or less consciously accepted certain features of the
Protestant world view, particularly Puritan capitalism.

In this group I should place England, Scotland,
the British Dominions, the United States and, off
to one side, Ireland. These countries now accept
Catholicism as a rich and powerful minority; they

24

tolerate and even esteem it, save for little factions and occasional antipapal outbursts like Orangeism in Ulster and Canada or the Ku Klux Klan and Blanshardism in the United States. The Faith is spreading steadily, thanks to conversions (especially in intellectual circles), those mixed marriages in which the non-Catholic spouse decides to enter the Church, and the higher Catholic birth rate in countries given over to contraception. The might of Catholicism lies not only in its homogeneity but in the quality of the faithful, who, generally, far surpass the members of other Christian denominations in assiduity. Furthermore, it holds a special attraction for certain groups within Protestantism—notably the High Church Anglicans of England and the Episcopalians of the United States. As a result, the Catholics in this Irish-Anglo-Saxon bloc feel a justifiable pride and enjoy a not unfounded sense of security; but at the same time, they seem a trifle too self-satisfied and tend to ignore the lessons of the past and the problems of the future while living entirely in a pretty comfortable present. They may also have some difficulty understanding the problems that often harass Catholics in other lands.

If we look closely, however, we see that this flourishing Irish-Anglo-Saxon group has problems of its own. Its increasing membership may be surpassing that of Protestant sects, which keep splitting into smaller communions, but it is threatened from both without and within by indifferentism and what American bishops have termed secularism. Danger lurks, too, in the social and cultural conformism rampant in Anglo-Saxon countries. Far more perilous is the subtle spell of semi-paganism disorienting and demoralizing many in the United States and England. To adduce but one instance of contamination, Catholic thinking in the United States has subscribed to oversimplified Freudian concepts which are now offered as representative of America's mentality. Each year, the Catholic Church in England and the United States chalks up conversions—sometimes striking ones; but, as some enter the Church, others silently slip out to wander in a miasma of indifference, and many others call themselves Catholics but think and live like their Protestant or unreligious neighbors.

In the last century, the Irish segment of this threefold community was preponderant. It remains important today, as can be seen in New York or in the valley of the Tyne. The reason is simple. Driven from their fatherland by misery, large well-knit groups of Irish Catholics emigrated under the guidance of their priests. Hard-working and enterprising, courageous and even belligerent, they possessed a staunch faith tempered by centuries of strife. To the Catholic communities of the Anglo-Saxon world, they brought their virtues—and their defects: a certain sentimentality peculiar to the

Celts and redirected by the Counter Reformation; a certain unawareness of intellectual problems; a certain tendency to lord it over others (a common reaction when a long-oppressed people regains its freedom); and, lastly, a certain insularity connected with that wondrous island, ultima Thule, at the very edge of the Western world.

It has been said that Catholics in the United States are insular for three reasons: because some are Irish, all are American and all are saturated with Anglo-Saxon culture. This is an exaggeration, of course, and can in no way form the basis for an evaluation of Catholicism in America. Equally unfair are the European standards applied by many hasty travelers. The example of Bishop Fulton J. Sheen, one of the greatest religious orators of the age, would alone refute their blanket judgments. No, Catholicism in the United States is solid, alive, generous: look at the heartwarming charities of the National Catholic Welfare Conference, the *Catholic Worker* and the famous shelter Dorothy Day and Peter Maurin opened in New York. It is often daring, too: observe the admirable work Father John La Farge, S.J., and Baroness de Hueck have been doing in the field of race relations. It is gradually acquiring what it once lacked in intellectual discipline: measure the influence wielded by Jacques Maritain, who is revered at Princeton and stupidly underrated in France. It is gaining spiritual depth also: study the writings of Thomas

Merton and see the many young men who are embracing the Trappists' life of silence. How foolish we should be to let yesterday's prejudices blind us to today's realities and tomorrow's possibilities!

The Catholic Church in England, on the other hand, seems to have withdrawn into herself since World War II. She is developing within her geographical boundaries, but she no longer speaks out to the world as in the days of Newman and Manning and Chesterton, that vital Titan who could have sat at board with Rabelais and Cervantes. She boasts talented writers like Evelyn Waugh, Bruce Marshall and the outstanding (if limited, controversial and sometimes dubious) novelist, Graham Greene. Although he was a truly remarkable essayist, the late Monsignor Ronald Knox—a convert, incidentally—failed to influence Western Europe as profoundly as did his predecessor, Monsignor Robert Hugh Benson, who is now so unjustly forgotten. In the past, Catholic England made many worthwhile contributions to the social sciences; today, however, except for Christopher Dawson in history and a few men like Michael Fogarty in economics, Catholic social teaching in England seems to have run out of ideas. Fresh views on economics are now coming to us from Colin Clark in Australia, who, though one of the greatest living economists, is more of a technician in economics than a thinker on social problems.

Ireland has even less contact with Catholicism on the Continent than England has. That is unfortunate for her and for us. Now that she has regained her independence, she is living in isolation—aloof even from England, her next-door neighbor. Her very population, now stationary, helps to deepen her isolationism; and former revolutionaries now in power, like Eamon de Valera, no longer come to the Continent for ideas and backing. As for us, too few Frenchmen or Germans or Italians know Ireland. Yet we could learn much from studying a nation where, apart from Ulster, there are no strictly religious subdivisions; where both citizens and state profess Catholicism; and where the people, conscious though they are of their psychological unity and mindful of Protestant England's persecutions, are so tolerant that they have not reclaimed old churches seized by the Protestants and have even elected a Jew as Lord Mayor of Dublin.

Lastly, we must consider the unique position of Catholics in South Africa, since that part of the world still belongs to the British Commonwealth of Nations. Catholics there encounter the racial hostility of Afrikaner governments, which are really Anglo-Boer systems influenced by a narrow and outmoded interpretation of Calvinism. Usually hidden in the embers, this animosity flares up whenever the faithful or the clergy denounce the policy of racial segregation that governments like those of Malan and Strijdom claim to have derived from the Bible. The Negroes, on the contrary, react as we should expect.

*

Next to the Irish-Anglo-Saxon bloc, related to it but nonetheless quite different, lies the Western European community, bound together by a common history of co-operation and war and by analogous geographical conditions. Just as we sometimes cannot see the forest for the trees, so we tend to concentrate on the differences between the Western European nations; but, striking and profound as those differences may be, they seem inconsequential when European Catholics meet in New York, Rio de Janeiro or Bombay, or convene for an international congress called by Rome.

This *Abendland* family includes the Netherlands, Belgium, Luxemburg, Western Germany, Austria, France, Switzerland and Italy—the northern half of Italy, that is: Turin, Milan, Genoa and Rome. The southern half exhibits qualities that place it in a class by itself. Included also is North Africa, by reason of the large European population of Tunisia, Algeria and Morocco. Spain, as we shall see, is a distant relative, much more closely bound to a definitely Iberian community; in fact, lying beyond the Pyrenees, she has never been and is not yet wholly European.

Denmark, Norway, Sweden, perhaps the northern part of the Netherlands and some sections of Germany—mainly the area about Kiel—form a little world of their own and very likely constitute the most dechristianized region in Europe. Protestantism is still the official religion there, but small sects are mushrooming. In the city, scarcely two per cent of the population practice, and the Lutheranism that holds sway in the country districts is often formalistic and hidebound. That it is not altogether dead, however, was proved by Carl Dreyer's film, *Ordet*. Industrial and commercial wealth together with a co-operative and corporative form of socialism creates a material prosperity that seems to encourage neurosis rather than thought. Artificial birth control is corrupting morals and decimating the population. Aided by tolerance, the Catholic Faith is moving back into Scandinavia after an absence of three hundred years. It has stirred some intellectual circles, as witnessed by the conversion of authors like Johannes Jörgensen and Sigrid Undset. The fact that Italians and Poles working there remain steadfast in the Faith suggests that they may do like Bruce Marshall's Irish and Italian laborers, who joined old Catholics in the Calvinistic Scotch Highlands and formed a parish for Father Smith.

Each Catholic community in Western Europe has its own traditions, characteristics and peculiarities which stand out in sharp contrast even when we compare dioceses that lie side by side on the map—as, for instance, Liège, Aix-la-Chapelle, Limburg in the Netherlands, Lyons, Geneva or Turin. This profusion of local differences distinguishes the Church in Western Europe from the Church in younger lands—say, in the United States.

But, important as the differences may be, the likenesses are even more fundamental. In the countries of the *Abendland* family, Christianity has its roots deep in very ancient peoples and cultures. To the tourist it is made visible in a long line of places of worship dating from the Catacombs and the great Roman basilicas to the church at Ronchamp, built by Le Corbusier, that pioneer of modern architecture. In like manner, the sometimes bewildering proliferation of movements and organizations and tendencies—especially in France —testifies to the complexity of historical influences and contributions, or, as American ethnologists say, patterns of culture. For example, in Pisa a pious confraternity vowed to burying persons who die as paupers dates back to the Middle Ages; at Avignon penitents garbed in gray or white still wear the cowl for solemn ceremonies; with headquarters in Rome, the Knights of Malta—founded a bit earlier than the Knights of Columbus—enjoy power and prerogatives which vex ecclesiastical and civil authorities.

32

To state the matter briefly, the Catholics of Europe are heirs to a long past, which is at once their strength and their weakness. Accordingly, they share in the strength and the weakness of Europe herself. They shine with her intellectual prestige but suffer from the resentment European domination has aroused. Rich when compared with underdeveloped peoples, they look almost poor, bankrupt and definitely lower-middle-class when compared with their brethren in the United States and Canada. Their very complexity makes it difficult for them to change, to reshape their familiar frame of reference, to strike out in new directions. Their traditions hold them together but constrict them, too—somewhat like mummy bands. No wonder Americans find this way of life "interesting," "quaint" and "picturesque" but too complicated and impractical. When, on a pilgrimage to Lourdes, the subjects of an American bishop gathered around to kiss his ring, he pushed them away with "That's not hygienic" and with the same gesture drew the boundary line between two worlds.

In Europe, intellectual considerations take first place. Sometimes, in fact, they take up too much place—as if every problem can be solved by a nice distinction, cogent oratory or a parroting of abstract principles. This is the besetting sin of the French, who, though not always logical, are logicians and grammarians at heart. Despite its penury in other spheres, Western Europe remains for the universal Church the constant wellspring of religious thought. Take Rome with its universities, the Gregorian, the Angelicum and so many others; Louvain, that ideally integrated university town; or Milan, with the University of the Sacred Heart; Paris, Lyons, Lille, Strasbourg; Nijmegen and the famous German universities. Even a partial enumeration like this proves that Europe is the center of intellectual life. So does a listing of Catholic publishers. Herder, in Fribourg-im-Brisgau; Desclée de Brouwer, in Belgium and France; Casterman, in Belgium; Editions du Cerf and Bloud et Gay, in France; Morcelliana, in Italy —all are important names. Among periodicals, whether specialized or of general interest, we have *Civiltà Cattolica, Etudes, La Vie Spirituelle, Herder Korrespondenz, Wort und Wahrheit* and *Nova et Vetera* (published at Fribourg in Switzerland). As for study groups, in France alone we can name the *Semaines sociales* (which have since been organized in more than twenty countries), *Economie et humanisme* and *L'Action populaire.* What shall we say of monumental projects like the Bollandist studies, Herder's dictionary, the *Dictionnaire de Théologie catholique,* Fliche's and Martin's *Histoire de l'Eglise* and the beautiful *Bible de Jérusalem?* And what of the numerous Catholic Action movements? The Continent has no monopoly on good works. We must recall that the Legion of

Mary was founded in Ireland; the Sword of the Spirit, in England; and the Christophers, in the United States. Still, the majority of such movements and organizations—even Jerusalem's center for Biblical studies—have their roots in Europe. This has nothing to do with the six-power agreement, the *C.E.C.A.*[1] or the common market; it is not a matter of Continental vanity, but of observable fact.

Because of Rome, which is the heart of the Church, and because of renowned shrines like Lourdes and Assisi, which draw pilgrims from everywhere, Europe is the center of the Catholic world—or, rather, surrounds the center as the pulp of fruit surrounds the stone. Europeans are conscious of the fact—perhaps too much so, just as Romans are apt to consider the papacy a mere adjunct to their *Urbs.* That lord-and-master attitude of Europeans is creating difficulties, especially now that, in the wake of World War II, the whole world is reacting against Europe, now that the Church must appear and be more universal than ever. The only solution would be for Europe, not to renounce her mission (for that would be false humility), but to admit that other Catholic communities, too, can develop and mature.

[1] The *C.E.C.A. (Communauté Européenne du Charbon et de l'Acier)* is an organization for the pooling of the coal and steel resources of France, Germany, Italy, Belgium, Holland and Luxemburg.—Tr.

Lastly, the Catholics of Europe are drawn together by another circumstance—this one purely historical and therefore transient: the proximity of Russian communism. In the northern and Germanic countries communism still seems a remote danger, whereas in the Latin countries it is the enemy within the gates. France and especially Italy both have a mighty communist machine with millions of voters to put party leaders in power at every election. Russian tanks wait only a few hundred kilometers from France; Russian rocket blasts directly threaten French soil; Russian-sponsored candidates obtained one out of every five votes in a recent French election. For the people of Western Europe, then, communism is not an abstraction, but a tangible reality; not a mere possibility, but both a menace and a temptation—and a source of anxiety either way. In this light we can understand the repeated warnings of religious authorities and their condemnation of communism and of those Catholics who lend it the *opera adjutrix* mentioned in the encyclical *Divini Redemptoris*. We can appreciate, too, the time and effort which thoughtful and energetic Catholics have expended clarifying their views on communism and communists, finding points of agreement or radical opposition, evaluating tactics and attitudes, and evolving apologetic and pastoral guides. We can see, furthermore, why they worked so intently in the Latin countries, France and the North of Italy, where communism has won over a considerable part of the working classes and is influencing the rest indirectly, and where most of the workers live as if there were no Church. The priest-worker movement may, for many reasons, have fallen short of its goal, but it was not unwarranted and it did try to answer very real and urgent needs.

Economically, the Catholic nations of Western Europe lie midway between the free enterprise of the United States and the rigidly organized economy of Russia. Theirs is a sort of unstable compromise between private and governmental capitalism, with farm districts remaining precapitalistic. This setup presents indubitable advantages and is well suited to individual economies that are too complex for centralization and too old for liberalism. But, like anything unstable, it hardly makes for a sense of comfortable security: from being perched on two rungs at once, it is unbalanced and always seems about to fall.

Although the Catholic communities of Europe have their roots deep in the past and sometimes glance back at it with nostalgia, sighing for "the age of belief" and "the faith of our fathers," they are also looking toward a future full of harrowing problems. And by preparing for that future, they escape the crushing weight of fatalism and defeatism. It is no accident that Catholic social thought in Western Europe is so probing, so bold and, at times, so imprudent. In the self-styled popular democracies, Catholics are not allowed to think. Except for the Negro and the Puerto Rican issues, as large a melting pot as the United States has no pressing social problem. Not so in Europe, and first of all in France.

But is France really so far ahead of other Catholic countries in the realms of thought and Catholic Action? Many Frenchmen think so, with a touch of naïve pride that warps their judgment. Convinced that God Himself is a Frenchman, they make their particular situation a pattern for the universe and ingenuously imagine that, as France grows, so grows humanity. It has not yet occurred to them that she no longer occupies the same position as before and just after the Revolution. Tomorrow's history will quite probably be made in New York and Moscow rather than in Paris or, certainly, Romorantin.

At the same time, Catholics from other lands, with fragmentary information and little understanding, exaggerate what they term the "crisis" of French Catholicism. What they diagnose as a crisis is often merely daring inquiry, overabundant and bungling energy or excessive reliance on Cartesian logic with its "clear and distinct" ideas. To keep the record straight, they would have to admit two facts: first, that French Catholics often grasp the nature of problems and do something about them before anyone else—though, unfortunately, they sometimes leave the follow-through to the less perceptive but more persevering; and, secondly, that the religious crisis caused by the upheaval of contemporary civilization is not a phenomenon peculiar to France, although it may be more acute and deeply felt there than elsewhere. But objectively, if the situation is to be called a crisis at all, it is one of growth in quantity and quality. Indeed, the renascence of French Catholicism is evident to anyone who compares the state of the Church in France today and at the turn of the century, when anticlericalist Emile Combes was in power and politico-religious questions were hotly debated. In this nation, which is demographically and economically sound but inclined to political disintegration, Catholicism—even though divided within—emerges as one of the few unimpaired forces, homogeneous and yet solid and flexible. Of all the countries of Western Europe, perhaps in France do Catholics manifest the keenest curiosity in the domain of thought and the most remarkable ingenuity in that of action. If the French achieve fewer and less impressive results than do Germans or Belgians, who are practicality itself, they have broader interests and find quicker solutions. No wonder the price of their gifts is a certain restlessness, febrility and impatience, an excessive fondness for wars of words and ideas. France has been called the eldest daughter of the Church, and she can be that forever provided she remembers that beyond her boundaries lies the rest of the world.

As I have said, Belgium and Germany are more practical, more persistent, more productive of results than France. It would be unjust, however, to limit their achievements to action. We cannot forget the decisive role Germany played in the liturgical revival thanks to the abbeys of Beuron and Maria-Laach, in the renewal of Biblical studies, and in outdoor and youth movements. Neither can we forget the world-wide Young Catholic Workers movement founded in Belgium by Canon Cardijn and Fernand Tonnet, or the outstanding work of liturgical education and missionary expansion accomplished by the Belgian Benedictine abbeys of Lophem, Mont-César and Maredsous. And we must mention such German intellectuals as Romano Guardini,[2] Reinhold Schneider and Gertrud von Le Fort, and such Belgians as Etienne de Greeff, Canon Leclercq and the Pleiad of Louvain whether at the University or at the Museum Lessianum, which is one of the intellectual centers of the Society of Jesus.

As the mere name of Chancellor Adenauer proves, Catholicism now holds an important place in Western Germany. No longer the minority

[2] The Newman Press has published two books by Msgr. Romano Guardini: *Meditations Before Mass* (1955) and *The Conversion of Augustine* (1960).—Tr.

religion against which Bismarck and Hitler waged their Kulturkampf, it was unexpectedly brought into the foreground by the division of Germany. Through the persecution and the perils they shared, the various confessions were taught to minimize if not to ignore their differences; so that the only opposition that perdures is the politico-religious opposition between Catholics and social-ists—and even that may lessen if Germany's evolu-tion parallels that of Austria, where, with a new-found sense of national community, Catholics and socialists are working together more closely.

Because of its biological and spiritual vitality, Catholicism is quietly and steadily gaining ground in countries that were once almost exclusively Protestant, like Switzerland and the Netherlands. The Dutch province of Limburg surely breaks the world record for the practice of religion; and, be-sides the spirit of methodicalness and meticulosity so typical of the Dutch, it has given the universal Church the most advanced thinking on the sub-ject of religious sociology. As for the Helvetic confederacy, the old central cantons of Fribourg and Valais are both traditionally and vitally Cath-olic; and the Church continues to gain in the large cities, starting with Geneva, once the capital of world Calvinism. Nevertheless, modern Switzer-land is not the force she was in Catholic thought during the last century with Python, Montenach and Decurtins, Cardinal Mermillod and the Cath-

41

olic Union for International Studies. In fact, she seems to be retiring somewhat into herself, settling down in the secure and sometimes dull sense of well-being engendered by her neutrality and the industry, equanimity and patriotism of her citizens.

Northern Italy was swept by a tidal wave of fascism and then almost entirely submerged in communism. Noisy and riotous as it was, fascism seems to have wreaked no profound damage on the mind and heart of the people, whereas the receding waters of communism disclose widespread devastation. Yet the Church in Italy defended herself vigorously and counterattacked without violence. Men of yesterday, like severe and loyal de Gasperi; and men of today, like smiling Giorgio La Pira, the redoubtable mayor of Florence, or Cardinal Lercaro, the apostle of Emilia—such men embody the Christian spirit of resistance to tyranny in any form. Some sections of Northern Italy are partly dechristianized, like Liguria with its capital, Genoa, and large industrial cities, such as Turin and Milan; others are extensively dechristianized, like Romagna and Emilia, which in no way resemble the little world of Don Camillo; yet, in others, the Faith, though perfectly traditional, is nonetheless lively and active—as, for example, in Venetia and in the radiant little city of Bergamo, a capital of Catholic Action. Southern Italy, poor, underprivileged and always somewhat colonial compared to the North, has not yet found herself. She has given Italians one of their foremost political philosophers in the person of Don Sturzo, theologian, sociologist and man of action; but she must work long and hard to discern and fulfill her destiny.

A coupler between the North and the South, Rome has its own problems, especially as regards its suburbs. But it cannot be treated as a mere geopolitical site: it transcends classification because it is the See of Peter and, as such, its catholicity outweighs its local and strictly Roman characteristics.

From Western Europe Catholicism has branched out to North Africa. Even with important sees like Carthage, Algiers and Rabat, the figure implicit in *branched* is only too accurate; for, despite the fact that conversions from Islam to Catholicism are more numerous than we think or hear of, they are still quite rare. Through men of action like Cardinal Lavigerie or contemplatives like Charles de Foucauld, our Faith has influenced but not superseded the rigorous or folkloric Islamism of North Africa. The Catholics there come from Europe— mostly from Corsica, Sicily and Malta, Spain and Portugal, Provence and Catalonia. The Maltese settlers are important in that, being Christians who speak a Semitic language, they are close to the Arabs and the Berbers and yet keep their own

43

faith as inexpugnable as their native land. To
some extent, the future of these Christian communities depends on the future of French colonial-
ism, but it seems likely that they will survive the
present crisis and bear witness to Christ in the
land of Islam. Groups of charitable and farsighted
Catholics in Morocco, Tunisia and even Algeria
have established a living link between the past and
the present, between Africa and Europe, between
Islam and the civilization that has sprung historically from Christianity.

*

Spain, after a fashion, has forged another such
link, although Generalissimo Franco's policies
have occasionally weakened it through inconsistency and the desire for immediate prestige.

With the mention of Spain we come to the
fourth bloc of Catholic countries—one of the most
extensive, most dispersed and now (without doubt)
most complex. They all use Spanish, which, along
with English, Russian and Chinese, is one of the
major languages today. Common to all is a background of Hispanicism—that is, a particular and
very original adaptation of the Latin element in
European culture. Concerning Church and state
and their mutual relations, they all entertain an
old notion to which time has added successive
alluvia, like the spirit of the Crusades and the
reconquista, memories of Spain's Golden Age un-

der Charles V, the acquisition of the West Indies, and the politico-religious totalitarianism of Philip II and his successors. Hence, they have long been inclined—and more so since Napoleon's invasion of Spain—to live in a dream of their glorious past and shut out the modern world, especially in all its "liberal" aspects.

No sooner have we stated these elementary truths than we stumble upon all manner of problems and complications. For example, can Portugal and her former dependency, the federal republic of Brazil, be neatly tucked away in one corner of what we call Iberia? Certainly not without bias and oversimplification. For one thing, Salazar is no Franco. For another, Brazil, being vigorous and full of young ideas, is far ahead of her neighbors to the north, south and west. The separation between Portugal and Brazil, moreover, was effected without the spirit of rebellion that animated Bolívar and San Martín. We should note the difference between both countries and stress the enormous potentialities hidden in the Amazon basin. Furthermore, Brazil has the advantage of being in contact with three families of nations— Iberian, American and European—without allowing herself to be absorbed by any of them. Her ability to synthesize while yet remaining original shines out when we examine the works of the puissant sociological thinker, Tristan de Athayde.

45

Another moot question: Exactly where should we fit borderline countries like the Philippines, Cuba, San Domingo and Puerto Rico, torn as they are between the Hispanic and the American ways of life?

How similar and yet dissimilar are such neighbors as Argentina, Chile, Uruguay and Paraguay! In some ways, Argentina looks more and more like the United States and has been traditionally democratic despite occasional dictators like Rosas and Juan Perón. Shoestring Chile is both rich and poor, more industrial than agricultural, and influenced by French and German ideas alike. Uruguay is a quiet and prosperous, democratic and liberal nation whose people are gradually returning to the Church from which they somewhat strayed. Predominantly Guaranian, Paraguay has never fully recovered from the insane wars waged by dictators Carlos Antonio López and his son.

Even within the tiny republics of Central America—scornfully dubbed "the Banana Republics" or "the United Fruit Company Empire"—an abyss separates democratic, Catholic and middle-class Costa Rica from poverty-stricken Panama and Guatemala.

Another question mark is Mexico, a country that has reverted to Aztecan ways and is governed by revolutionaries as conservative now as the leaders they once overthrew.

Still, certain factors unite all these Latin American countries, whether they be of Spanish or Portuguese background. They manifest serious social and political instability because of their rapid and uncontrolled economic growth. They frequently experience restlessness or violent turmoil in the fascist or communist manner. They are subjected to virulently anti-Catholic propaganda by the Protestant Churches of the United States and missionary sects like the Jehovah's Witnesses. They suffer from a critical shortage of priests, as shown by the fact that in Venezuela a bishop may have to trinate every Sunday. They are suddenly awakening to religion, and the best Catholics among them are dedicating themselves unreservedly to apostolic and social work, regardless of certain groups which obstinately cling to the old order—or disorder. In short, the atmosphere is one of ebullience, a thick bubbling up of ideas and words and deeds.

These Latin Americans possess immense good will but often lack the intellectual or material means to carry through. Their eagerness and laudable intentions are echoed in the excellent periodical called *Criterio*. Founded in Buenos Aires by Bishop Franceschi and read throughout Spanish

47

America, this review has collaborators from all over the world and, of today's many Catholic journals, presents what is perhaps the broadest picture of world Catholicism.

Agitation does not make for clarity. Accordingly, the position of Spanish-speaking Catholics in America is complicated and confusing. So too in Spain, where the apparent uniformity imposed by Franco merely hides the complexity from outsiders.

Spain is Castile; but it is Andalusia, Catalonia and the Basque region, too—together with distinctive varieties of Catholicism, more sharply divided and even antipodean than all the sections of France. Spain holds two kinds of Catholics: the first, satisfied with Franco and his regime, ask no questions, suspend their judgment and mouth marvelous principles that need only be applied; the second, daring and courageous, ask plenty of questions and, like the Bishops of Malaga and Cordova, try to answer them as well as possible. Spain is a multitude of persons who concentrate on national and even provincial particularism. Yet, she is also a nation of remarkable debaters, who influence what may be called the "international class." Outstanding among these is Carlos Santamaria, the founder of the Conversations of San Sebastian.

The more familiar Spain becomes to me—especially Catholic Spain—the more her violent con-

trasts and her bewildering complexity both fasci-
nate and disconcert me. Ten years ago I could
write, without exaggeration, that the Catholicism
of the Iberian bloc looked to the past rather than
the future or even the present. Today, such an
assertion would be false and, what is worse, unjust.
Remember Cervantes, Lope de Vega, Fray Luis de
León, Francisco de Vitoria, Saint John of the Cross
and Saint Teresa of Avila, and you sense what
Iberian Catholicism could offer the world.

*

We come now to the last family of Churches—if,
indeed, we may call it a family at all. It comprises
the new Catholic communities of Africa and Asia,
some of them descended from very ancient
Churches (like the Chaldean in Iraq and the Syro-
Malabar in India), but the majority of them derived from more recent ones created by missionaries during the last three centuries and notably
since the time of Saint Francis Xavier. This group
has just begun its evolution. The newest and most
promising within the Catholic Church, it is also
the least homogeneous and the least certain. On
looking at it, we wonder what its members have
in common. First, they are all colored, though that
term covers many shades and tints. Next, they are
all experiencing the vast reawakening which was
caused by Europe's colonial expansion and is now
(especially since the talks at Bandung) at the stage
of decolonization. Lastly, they spring from the an-

cient civilizations of the Orient or the "traditional" ones of Africa; and for that reason, they are alien to the civilization and culture of Europe and to its prolongation in the United States and Russia.

These common bonds are strong, particularly now, but let us not forget that they are negative and provisional. Someday the peoples of Africa and Asia will assert their individual originality with regard to one another just as they now defend their common originality from encroachment by European, American or Russian civilization.

Be that as it may, the presence of these new Catholic communities at international congresses glows like a reality and a promise for the future. What an unforgettable experience it is to hear Indian-born Archbishop Gracias of Bombay, or Doctor John C. H. Wu, who combines Chinese wisdom with his knowledge of Western culture! And behind them we see the teeming multitudes they represent. Among the Negro leaders in Africa, N'Krumah of Ghana, M'Bida of Cameroun, Azango of Hazouma and Apithy of Dahomey are Catholics; so is Ngo-Dinh-Diem of Vietnam; and a Jesuit, Father D'Souza, has filled an important political post in India. Such facts should make us proud—and a bit anxious, too, as we wonder whether we can shoulder the responsibilities they place upon us. When the organizers of France's

Semaines sociales hear that similar meetings are now held in Japan, they see that the reality has far surpassed their dreams.

These Catholic communities encounter similar problems and must perform analogous feats to solve them. They must guard against the encroachment of Western culture while yet assimilating everything they need in it, especially science and technology and (what is more difficult) the mentality which makes scientific know-how and technical efficiency possible. They need to baptize and purify their local allegiances lest these degenerate into narrow nationalism. They should retain what is truly human in their patriotism and reject what is anti-human and anti-Christian. They have to repulse communism and actively contribute to the economic and social progress their countries so sorely need. Despite differences of landscape and psychology, these same conditions obtain in Japan and Lebanon, in Togo and Natal.

Still, we must take the differences into account. The Copts of Nasser's Egypt, for example, the Maronites of Lebanon and the Armenians of Syria have been Christian communities since long before the Germans or the English. The Catholics who clung to their faith in Nagasaki and the Vietnamese who have survived three centuries of persecution are, in a way, ancient Christians. The Negroes of Uganda and Cameroun and South Africa, on

51

the contrary, we may call new Christians. Now, as we all know, patriarchs and neophytes have neither the same spirit nor the same problems.

Some of these newly established or reconstituted nations have absorbed certain features of Western culture through England, Spain, Portugal or France. Thus, among these international blocs, there has spontaneously arisen a fairly well-defined "French alliance," which regroups the capital and its overseas territories, recently liberated colonies like Vietnam and even French-speaking Canada, Belgium, the French sector of Switzerland, the Belgian Congo, Haiti, Lebanon and parts of Syria, Egypt and Ethiopia. Diverse as they are, these countries often achieve instinctive agreement and understanding. It seems that France with her culture has created between them a stronger intellectual bond than has England with both her culture and her language.

Other differences which we must take into consideration depend on the stage of historical development these various Christian communities have reached. For some are ancient and in the process of renewal, such as those in the Near East, Vietnam or South Korea; others, like those in Equatorial or Central Africa, have been bound by tradition and are trying to catch up with history. Some are completely independent; others—say, Ghana and Cameroun—are independent in theory but quite dependent in fact; others yet, like Madagascar, are seeking autonomy. Some are well-endowed industrially and economically, as Japan has always been; others, such as Lebanon, have made economic progress but are still underdeveloped in some areas; and other again are backward, like most of those in Asia and Africa.

The presence of this Afro-Asian bloc in the structure and the councils of the Church militant is the most striking innovation of our age. Now more than ever the Church is catholic—a universal assembly. And we are just beginning. As has been said, we are the first Christians.

*

One last point. In the history of the Church there have always been countries that shared in several cultures, served as a common meeting ground for them and united them in a spirit of brotherhood. One of these countries was Switzerland at the end of the last century, thanks especially to the University of Fribourg. Another was Belgium between both World Wars. Though small, both countries had big hearts, and, at a time when Europe was thinking and acting in behalf of the whole Church, they effectually united Catholics of Germanic and Latin origin. Not so today. Belgium and Switzerland now have a purely European mission.

53

I may be mistaken but, now that lightning transportation and communications have shrunk the world, I discern several countries which could—and, to a certain extent, already do—serve as hinges or common meeting places throughout Christendom.

One such is Poland. The only "popular democracy" in which the Church possesses a modicum of freedom, Poland is both Slavic and Latin, and, consequently, could link the Slavic world with the Teutonic and the Latin, and the capitalistic world with the communistic. For this task the people of Poland are eminently qualified because of their plasticity and their affability, their linguistic aptitudes and their staunch faith.

Then there is French Canada. Highly original, necessarily bilingual and traditionally pacific, she keeps a sharp eye on Europe—France, in particular—and the United States. She could, therefore, bridge the gap between European and American culture, between the Catholics of Western Europe and those of the Irish-Anglo-Saxon group. The elite of Canada are aware of her mission.

Another hinge-country would be Argentina, which speaks Spanish, welcomes French thought and works within an almost American economic system. Geography has made her a necessary clear-

inghouse for ideas. As for Brazil, I have already
spoken of her vocation.

Lebanon rightly wants to be the Switzerland of
the Near East—a nexus between the Occident and
the Orient, the Arab world and the European. Together with Israel, perhaps, she could be the spiritual stronghold of the Mediterranean. Such also is
the geographic role of ancient Phoenicia. And let
us not ignore the part nearby Antioch can play in
the growth of the Church.

As far as Asia is concerned, I am not so sure.
Now that Japan has shaken off imperialism, the
suppleness of her people, their urbanity and their
power of assimilation as well as their relations with
Europe and America may fit her to be a vinculum
between East and West.

*

With these vistas I complete my geography of
contemporary Catholicism. I could have called it a
"geography of the heart," for it was written from
the heart of a Catholic who, wherever he has gone,
has met other hearts that were united to his in
brotherhood.

chapter three

A Spectral Analysis

of

Contemporary Catholicism

At the beginning of Sunday Mass not too long ago, some of my readers may have been handed a questionnaire and a pencil to fill it out. Whenever and wherever this was done, they understood that they were co-operating in a religious census which would aid statistical studies in sociology and pastoral theology. Their work facilitated the writing of this chapter.

From France, where it originated with Gabriel Le Bras and Canon Boulard, research in religious sociology soon spread throughout Christendom, so much so that it almost seems a fad, and all we hear of today is inquiries, censuses and polls. The fact is that these methods do not tell the whole story and cannot convert the world. They do, however, suggest where the truth may be found, dispel prejudice, corroborate intuitions, deepen understanding and permit more intelligent action.

Such investigations seek to answer the question posed in the title *France, pays de missions?* When this famous little book by Fathers Godin and Daniel appeared in 1943, the information it offered on Paris and its suburbs stirred the interest, the emotions and the will of apostolic souls. No longer could they be satisfied with opinions and approximations; they wanted facts, cold and precise, and consequently adopted scientific methods and developed the field of religious sociology.

It is because of their findings that I dare attempt the analysis contained in this chapter—an analysis that pertains to both demography and sociology. Just as a prism separates a ray of white light into the seven principal colors of the spectrum, so, having listed the geographic components of the Church, I shall now try to resolve contemporary Catholicism into its demographic and sociological elements. Unfortunately, the very nature of analysis forces me to draw and quarter the living reality I am studying. When this chapter is over, I shall have explained everything—without having explained anything very profoundly, much like the master weaver who, to examine a fabric, must tear it apart and so make it lose its body and its sheen. In short, we shall have to wait till later for a living synthesis.

*

If we scrutinize contemporary Catholicism in the light of demographic principles, we shall be struck by the difference between underdeveloped countries and those that boast industrial progress and large cities.

In the more privileged countries the vigor of Catholic life assures the Faith a remarkably steady progress. Their birth rate alone would keep Catholics constantly growing in number. Thus it is in countries where Protestants predominate or represent a strong minority and where Neo-Malthusianism is gradually decimating the Calvinistic or Lutheran middle classes—as, for instance, in the Netherlands, Switzerland, England, the United States, Australia, New Zealand and parts of Canada. In these "birth-control countries" Catholicism is winning what French Canadians call "the battle of the cribs." The Neo-Malthusian mentality has contaminated Catholics, too, but not as generally as it has the indifferent or those outside the Church. As a result, the traditional ratio of Protestants to Catholics has been reversed in many regions.

The same phenomenon often occurs in once Catholic countries that have since drifted into religious indifference. Here in France, if I may cite a few examples, many regions that have strayed from the Faith have also become dehumanized and devitalized—regions like Creuse, Haute-Vienne, Yonne and certain parts of the Southwest. On the other hand, many but not all traditionally Catholic sections maintain a high birth rate. Outstanding among those that do are Vendée and certain *départements* of Brittany. In the cities, the large, prosperous families founded by Catholics who live their beliefs stand in telling contrast to the childless or one-child homes of those who are indifferent, though they may wear a mask of religiosity. I think it significant that the members of the Popular Republican Movement have the most children of any group in Parliament and that the radicals and the socialists have the least. The spirit behind birth control has erected an invisible but unsurmountable barrier between Catholics and non-Catholics.

In most of these countries, nevertheless, Catholicism continues to be the bulwark of sound family values: the unity, the indissolubility and the fecundity of marriage; a true understanding of love; and a sexual and familial morality which is strict but untainted by the Puritanical or Jansenistic notions that held sway from the seventeenth century to the beginning of the twentieth. It is no accident that the present world-wide efforts to safeguard the family originated in France with social thinkers like Paul Bureau, Edouard Jordan, Auguste Isaac, Father Viollet and Emmanuel Gounot. Neither is it an accident that the most effective plan for economic aid to families was devised by a Catholic, Emile Romanet, of Grenoble. Rereading the encyclicals *Arcanum divinae* by Leo XIII and *Casti connubii* by Pius XI and allocutions to engaged couples and newlyweds by Pius XII will convince us that such matters are not left to chance.

The facts stated so far could inspire imprudent optimism unless we also considered the underdeveloped countries (which happen to be mostly pagan or Moslem) and saw that there the situation is shockingly reversed. I shall not mention Latin America or the few parts of Africa that have already been converted to Catholicism. Elsewhere, the Faith is the possession of more or less important minorities which, though fertile, are not more so and are sometimes much less so than the masses where procreation is still regulated by instinct and custom. Numerous as conversions may be, missionary work cannot keep pace with the birth rate. Such is the situation in nearby North Africa as well as in China and India, those enormous womb-lands of humanity. This losing battle could discourage and torment an apostle who dreams of winning the world to Christ, yet most Christians do not even realize what is going on.

The laws of demography, then, work both for and against Catholicism; but in the long run, they work against it insofar as the number of pagans or Moslems exceeds that of peoples which were once Christian. Despite its importance in comparison with other creeds, Catholicism is already a minority religion, and the sheer number of pagans and Moslems seemingly threatens to make it ever more

61

so. But, for two reasons, that is not necessarily true. First, it appears likely that Neo-Malthusianism will sooner or later contaminate the masses of Africa and Asia. In fact, bizarre "missionaries" of the American way of life are busily disseminating birth-control information right now, and Red China cannot decide whether to lower her birth rate or dominate by sheer numbers. Secondly, intellect and free will can outmaneuver blind determinism. If the faithful heed the voice of the spirit, their large, happy, vigorous families will beget a multitude of apostles—whether lay, religious or priestly—and nurture a missionary zeal which can enkindle the whole world.

*

Demography and religious sociology further prove that, often, our religious services draw more women than men, and more children and old persons than adults. Considering differences of place and time, the proportion of each may be normal or abnormal. It is normal if, in a given district, there are more women than men; or if, in a country which is getting back on its feet demographically, like France, the adults are not nearly so numerous as the young or the old. It is abnormal if the adult male population, though present, is worth next to nothing. When that happens, religion is divorced from manliness and made a matter of age or sex, as in many country districts of France, Italy, Spain and Portugal. In numerous

European cities, however, more men are practicing their religion today than during the last century, when church-going in the city was restricted almost exclusively to women. The situation has changed, and in some places the men practice better than the women, as often happens when dechristianized throngs reawaken to religion.

From these facts we see that the practice of religion can vary from one place to another, even in areas where the Catholic Church is very old and very firmly established. According to inquiries and statistics, the proportion of practicing Catholics runs from one hundred per cent or nearly so in Southern Holland, Westphalia, some cantons of Alsace or Vendée or Brittany and certain towns of Venetia, through every figure imaginable down to near or absolute zero in Saxony and Jutland, some outlying *départements* of France's Massif Central, the South of Portugal, certain districts of Spain, and individual villages in Romagna and Emilia.

Both extremes appear especially in country districts, where conformity and human respect carry more weight than in the city. The proportion of practicing Catholics in cities neither soars very high nor plunges very low: in large cities—except in Scandinavian countries—it rarely exceeds thirty per cent or dips below ten. Even then, these general estimates must be modified. Within Paris, for instance, there are two cities living side by side, so to speak: one, a middle-class city where practicing Catholics average twenty-five to thirty per cent of the population; the other, a proletarian city where they sometimes fall below two per cent. In London, Newcastle, New York and Chicago, Catholics attend church far more assiduously than do Protestants—even Methodists and others who were so zealous during the last century.

These figures and comparisons evoke two pictures: in France and Portugal, magnificent Gothic or Romanesque churches, still standing but almost empty; and, in the suburbs or recently developed sections of modern cities, new churches or chapels already overflowing with worshipers. Both pictures, along with the figures and the graphs, reveal the complexity of today's Catholicism, which blends the most ancient traditions and the most modern innovations. They also prove that Christianity, far from progressing uniformly, comes to a standstill or even loses ground in some places and elsewhere sweeps ahead. While one locality lies torpid, another rises from sleep, and still another springs up from nowhere, bright as a star that has just come into view. Whatever they are, these mysterious differences result from material conditions, free will and grace.

*

We also have statistics on how many priests and religious men and women there are per thousand faithful. What strikes us, again, is the wide diversity of figures. Southern Holland, for example, produces so many priests and religious men and women that she can send them into the whole world without ever running short. At the other end of the scale we find areas like those in Central America, Catholic in name but in fact dechristianized, where there is only one priest for twenty thousand inhabitants. In countries where several religions prevail, we arrive at the correct proportion by dividing the number of priests into the total population, Catholic or not, since the Church cannot find it in her heart to abandon anyone. Incidentally, the French tend to exaggerate their need for priests. In point of fact, they are one of the most fortunate groups, having one priest—and even more religious women—per seven or eight hundred inhabitants. The scarcity of priests they speak of is, therefore, relative and depends on conditions within each diocese. To tell the truth, theirs is a problem, not of numbers, but of redistribution and use. It is annoying, when you think of it, to hear France beg for priests from other countries when so many of these are less richly endowed than she—but, then, few French Catholics can see beyond home to the universal Church. I do not mean, of course, that France has too many priests: indeed, those she has hardly suffice to cope with her urgent and ever-growing needs; and, to make matters worse, there has been an alarming drop in priestly vocations in the past few years.

In short, except for a few privileged areas, there is a general dearth of priests and religious. In some localities, the shortage is relative; in others, absolute. It is almost always painful; and when apostolic zeal grows stronger and thinking Catholics yearn for a deeper spiritual life, it is sometimes tragic.

*

From a social viewpoint, Marxists and even certain Catholics maintain that the Church is linked with capitalism and the *bourgeoisie*. Even at first sight, their verdict seems hasty and simplistic; on further examination, it proves quite unjustified, based as it is on *a priori* judgments and ill-considered extrapolations prompted by incomplete observation.

On the whole, the millionaire set in the financial and business world can hardly be labeled Catholic even in countries in which Catholicism is the chief religion, as in France. It numbers far more Protestants, Jews and indifferentists than Catholics. Rockefeller and Henry Deterding, the petroleum tycoons; Andrew Carnegie, the steel king; Pierpont Morgan, the banker; Basil Zaharoff; Alfred Krupp, the munitions magnate; or, of course, the Rothschilds, the lords of finance for half a century—none of these men were Catholics. Even in France, Jews and Protestants (or Protestant High Society, as the French say) play a comparatively more important role in business than in the rest of the country's life. As for the "bourgeois dynasties" begotten by the French Revolution, most may have had Catholic antecedents but they began by declaring themselves anticlerical and Voltairian; later, as the French leftist party became less anticlerical and more socialistic, some drew closer to Catholicism, but their religion has often shown itself utilitarian and social rather than profound and vital. In general and just about everywhere, the millionaire class has developed either outside of Catholicism, as have the Jews and the Protestants; or against it, like the plunderers of national assets during the French Revolution or like Cavour and Crispi in their liberalized Italy. This is particularly evident in Belgium, whose liberal party is anticlerical and capitalistic; and in Alsace and certain sectors of Switzerland, where bourgeois Protestants engaged in business are superposed over Catholics, whether these be peasants, laborers or members of the middle classes.

Still in all, there are in the business world some truly Catholic families whose lives are actuated by faith. To cite a well-known example, Count Chandon-Moët, one of the most important names in France's champagne industry, was, along with Léon Harmel, a leader in the Catholic social awakening. Then there is the mayor of Naples, Achille Lauro. We may deem this ship-owner's politics too monarchistic or find his social-mindedness smacks of demagoguery, but we cannot doubt the sincerity of his faith. To sum up this part of our discussion, we may safely assert that Catholics are few and far between in the world of millionaires.

*

Having said that, we still have not disproved the Marxists' allegation for the simple reason that this millionaire group, despite its qualitative importance, is a mere fraction of the *bourgeoisie*.

Matters are quite different in the upper middle classes—that is, in that part of the *bourgeoisie* made up of civic and military leaders, landowners in the manner of the old aristocracy, skilled technologists, intellectuals, professionals, and the managers and executive staffs of large public and private organizations. The religious life of these several bourgeois groups has varied enormously from generation to generation and still does according to locality.

In the regions which remained Catholic after the Reformation, the *haute bourgeoisie* of civic and military leaders comprises many Catholic families whose religious life ranges from habit and convention to deep personal conviction. Thus it is with certain French families which have produced long lines of military men, magistrates and mem-

68

bers of the Council of State. Men like Castelnau, Franchet d'Esperey, Leclerc and Charles de Gaulle are typical of one such group in France. Analogous remarks could be made about Belgium and Italy. In the past, these groups manifested a leaning toward Jansenism—or, rather, toward a Jansenistic brand of Puritanism—which they have since repudiated. In Protestant countries the same groups belong to the reformed Churches.

The same cleavage appears in the landowning group within the upper middle classes (I should say: in what is left of that fast-disappearing race). For the most part—and this is true especially in the West, in Vendée and Brittany—France's wealthy landowners profess the Faith of their ancestors somewhat in the style of the peasants, whereas the landed gentry across the Channel adhere to the Church of England and look on the High Church's ritualism with distrust.

Managers and executives constitute a new category. As they have risen from the middle classes by way of renowned engineering institutes, they are more amenable to the principles of renascent Catholicism than are bourgeois businessmen. Furthermore, though these executives must obey the laws of efficiency and production, they are not as profit-minded as are capitalists strictly so-called. It is not surprising, then, to find among executives in France and elsewhere many Catholics who sincerely want to insure social justice and improve management-personnel relations.

*

So notable is the religious contribution of many intellectuals today that it deserves a study all to itself.

Gone are the days when intellectuals banded together against the Church, when hardly a writer or a thinker dared defend her publicly. Today, every field of research, creativity and teaching is filled with countless Catholic intellectuals, some of whom have earned an international reputation. Naturally, they must reckon with other schools of thought, like liberalism, which still enthralls its votaries; Marxism, although its prestige is waning of late; the existentialism of Heidegger or Sartre; more or less socialistic or nationalistic forms of positivism that have remained with us; and the sheer nihilism, the universal spirit of revolution, analyzed by Albert Camus in *L'Homme révolté*. But the very adversaries of Catholicism now acknowledge the merit of its exponents.

To ascertain their merit, we need only name a few converts at random. In the sciences, we can mention Charles Nicolle and Victor Grignard, Nobel Prize winners in medicine and chemistry respectively; Alexis Carrel; Karl Stern, one of to-

70

day's foremost psychiatrists; and Pierre Lecomte du Noüy, who is both a mathematician and a physicist. In literature, an array of writers like Léon Bloy, Max Jacob, Evelyn Waugh, Sigrid Undset, Johannes Jörgensen, Maurice Baring, Charles Plisnier and Giovanni Papini; and poets like Francis Jammes, Paul Claudel, Gertrud von Le Fort and Charles Péguy.[1] In art, sculptor Eric Gill and painters like Georges Desvallières, Albert Gleizes and Georges Rouault. In history, Reinhold Schneider, Daniel-Rops and Gaston Roupnel. In criticism, Theodor Haecker, Gustave Cohen, Charles du Bos and this age's outstanding Hellenist, Gilbert Murray. In philosophy, Jacques Maritain,[2] Gabriel Marcel, Henri Bergson, Hugo Ball and Edith Stein,[3] who became a Carmelite and died in a concentration camp. In sociology, Arnaud Dandieu has done brilliant work. Many do not fit into any of these categories—for example, Paul Misraki with his songs; Dorothy Day, that admirable American writer and journalist who has fought so courageously for social justice and Cath-

[1] For an account of Péguy's conversion as well as a study of his works, see *Charles Péguy: The Pursuit of Salvation* by Yvonne Servais (Westminster, Maryland: The Newman Press, 1953).—Tr.

[2] Maritain's conversion is well analyzed in *The Philosophy of Jacques Maritain* by Charles Fecher (The Newman Press, 1953).—Tr.

[3] See *The Scholar and the Cross: The Life and Work of Edith Stein* by Hilda C. Graef (The Newman Press, 1955); and *Writings of Edith Stein*, selected and translated with an introduction by Hilda C. Graef (The Newman Press, 1956).—Tr.

71

olic Action; Marcelle Auclair, the greatest French journalist of this generation; my friend H. C. E. Zacharias, who has been biologist, planter, ethnologist and historian successively; and, again, Dumoulin, the former secretary-general of France's General Confederation of Labor, and Chastenet, once a socialist deputy, both of whom are excellent writers.

Especially significant, I think, is the conversion of two French intellectuals I knew who both wanted to die within the Church. The first, destined to be shot after the Liberation, was Jean Luchaire, one of the most untroubled pagans I have ever met. The other, Marcel Déat, was a socialist and a sociologist in the tradition of Dürkheim, rabidly anticlerical all through life. Face to face with death and stripped of their masks, both of them knelt before Christ and His Church. It is no less significant that *The Bells of Nagasaki*, written by a Catholic Japanese doctor, is the most popular book in Japan and a best seller throughout the world.

These dazzling constellations of converts should not blind us to the splendid intellectuals who were born in the Church. The genius of Bergson and Maritain cannot dim that of Maurice Blondel, a thinker whose faith never wavered for an instant, or of Emmanuel Mounier, the philosopher of involvement,[4] who practiced what he preached and was the inspiration of contemporary personalism. Once again, so many names spring to mind that we have to pick only a few here and there: [5] in exegesis, Marie-Joseph Lagrange; [6] in history, Jules Lebreton, Augustin Fliche, René Grousset, Christopher Dawson and Schnürer; in theology, Yves Congar,[7] Henri de Lubac,[8] Hugo Rahner,[9] Karl Rahner [10] and Hans Urs von Balthasar; [11] in science, geologist Teilhard de Chardin, phonetician *abbé* Rousselot and mathematician Francisco Severi; in sociology, Paul Bureau, Luigi Sturzo and Goetz Briefs; in economics, Colin Clark and François Perroux; in philosophy, Antonin Sertillanges,[12] Gustave Thibon and Jacques

[4] Mounier's characteristic term is *engagement,* an almost untranslatable word which suggests, not mere commitment, but devotion and dedication so wholehearted that it involves the whole man.—Tr.

[5] For the reader's convenience, I shall list in the appropriate place all the works which The Newman Press has published by the authors named in the text.—Tr.

[6] Marie-Joseph Lagrange, O.P.: *The Gospel of Jesus Christ* (1943).

[7] Yves M.-J. Congar, O.P.: *Christ, Our Lady and the Church* (1957); *Lay People in the Church* (1957); and *Theology of the Church* (1959).

[8] Henri de Lubac, S.J.: *Further Paradoxes* (1958).

[9] Hugo Rahner, S.J.: *The Spirituality of St. Ignatius of Loyola* (1953); and *The Parish: From Theology to Practice* (1958).

[10] Karl Rahner, S.J.: *Happiness Through Prayer* (1958); and *Encounters with Silence* (1960).

[11] Hans Urs von Balthasar: *Science, Religion and Christianity* (1959).

[12] Antonin G. Sertillanges, O.P.: *The Intellectual Life* (1959).

Chevallier. If we did not stop here, the list would run on endlessly; and even if it did, it would be incomplete and, consequently, unfair.

One example will summarize what I have been saying. Before the Second World Congress of the Lay Apostolate held in Rome, the committee in charge published a book of previews, so to speak, which was translated into several languages under titles meaning *The World Is Awaiting the Church.* Without further commentary, the list of authors who collaborated on the volume proves my point. Among them were:

> jurist Vittorino Veronese, of Italy;
>
> diplomat, author and journalist Wladimir d'Ormesson, of France;
>
> statesman Dr. Konrad Adenauer, of Germany;
>
> Secretary of the nation's Social Welfare Department Dr. Marga A. M. Klompe, of Holland;
>
> jurist and statesman Kotaro Tanaka, of Japan;
>
> jurist and statesman Raymond Scheyven, of Belgium;
>
> jurist and mayor Giorgio La Pira, of Florence, Italy;
>
> jurist Dr. John C. H. Wu, of China;
>
> historian and expert on the philosophy of history Christopher Dawson, of England;

former Vice-President of the Republic Dr.
John M. Chang, of Korea; [13]

King Mutara III, of Ruanda-Urundi;

mathematician Francesco Severi, of Italy;

psychiatrist Karl Stern, of Austria and
Canada;

medical doctor J. J. Lopez Ibor, of Spain;

labor leader and president of the AFL-CIO
George Meany, of the United States;

architect Hermann Baur, of Switzerland;

motion picture actress Ann Blyth, of the
United States;

engineer Gustave Corçao, of Brazil;

novelist Bruce Marshall, of Scotland;

poet and novelist Gertrud von Le Fort, of
Germany;

and Joseph Folliet, whom you will please excuse me for not introducing.

This partial list of contributors is interesting for
three reasons: it demonstrates at a glance the
catholicity of the Church, the presence of Catholic intellectuals in the world today, and the spirit
of dedication behind their activity. In whatever
field these scholars, writers and professors work,
they cannot help influencing intellectual circles
everywhere, from groups of teachers, lawyers and

[13] Dr. Chang was elected Premier of South Korea's Second
Republic on August 19, 1960.—Tr.

doctors down to the young men and women in our schools and colleges. For proof as well as signs of wonders to come, we need but look around. Catholic students now outnumber all others in Paris' Ecole polytechnique, once the stronghold of unbelieving positivism. Every year, thousands of school people from Paris commemorate Charles Péguy's pilgrimage to Chartres. The Newman Clubs in British and American universities urge young minds to search for truth and unity. Italy's *studenti* and *laureati* effectively consolidate pupils and young professionals, and Spain's *Opus Dei* attracts many students.

But let not our optimism carry us away. In such matters, nothing is simple; above all, nothing is definite. For example, statistics may indicate whether a collegian performs his Easter duties, but they cannot gauge the character and the intensity of his spiritual life. While some intellectuals enter or re-enter the Church, others leave through hostility or indifference. Granted that Catholic organizations are recruiting an impressive portion of the educated class, still not all these are equally vital or suited to the needs of the day. And as for Catholic intellectuals themselves, some are tormented by excruciating problems—a few of which we shall discuss in subsequent chapters.

Without undue optimism we can close this section by saying that the Faith is a living force in intellectual circles. Its cogency comes partly from the clear and coherent solutions the unshakable Church offers to today's problems; partly from the breakdown of all the ideologies evolved in the nineteenth century; but largely, and perhaps especially, from the fact that religion in urban areas is no longer a matter of routine and social convention but of deliberate choice which commits the whole man. Now, unless they degenerate into mere technicians in some specialty or other, intellectuals are best fitted by their work to appreciate those solutions and make that choice.

*

Rural districts present quite another picture. Traditionally, country dwellers look to the past and are governed by custom. As demonstrated in the works of France's Henri Pourrat, Italy's Ignazio Silone and England's Thomas Hardy, the religion of country people is frequently (though less and less so nowadays) bound up with certain secular traditions. Hence it is that some Protestant countries, like England, have very few Catholics living in rural areas and practically none among the actual peasantry. Likewise in the United States, except in rare, well-determined regions like the New England states, where Franco-American farmers from Canada often replaced "the Yankees"; and in California, where the impress of Spanish colonization remains profound. Quite the opposite holds true of Catholic countries. There are almost no Protestant farmers in Italy, for instance, except for a few Waldensians near the Alps; and none at all in Spain or Latin America. On the other hand, those parts of Latin America peopled by Indians have created new traditions out of a more or less successful symbiosis of the Catholic Faith and local customs and beliefs. The Catholicism of the Peruvian Indians, to cite but one case, has been strongly colored by their age-old traditions.

Yet, we should err if we thought the rural areas of Catholic countries were necessarily pledged to Catholicism. The religious geography of France's country districts clearly illustrates every degree of religious life between complete dechristianization and total adherence to the Faith. In the old Catholic countries, the Church sometimes covered immemorial paganism with a thin coat of paint; but when she attempted to transform it more deeply, she was opposed by the cities, which, with the eighteenth century, became centers of belligerent unbelief. Since the industrial revolution, furthermore, city life has been luring people away from the country and ever more profoundly influencing those who have remained there. These conditions explain, in part, the varying degrees of religious life observable in country districts. Traditional Catholicism has held on most tenaciously in those sections—like the West of France—which were evangelized fairly recently with systematic vigor and persistence. The paradox is only apparent. In those traditionally Catholic areas, as well as in more or less dechristianized ones, there is arising a new type of peasant or rural Catholic—one who fuses "traditional" religion and "personal" religion into a living synthesis. This phenomenon, one of the most striking achievements of Catholic Action, began in France with the Young Catholic Farmer movement [14] and is now spreading throughout the world—even Africa, where converted Negro farmers are performing the miracles that will bring them forward from archaic to modern rural life.

*

Middle-class groups are naturally conservative and deliberately conformist. Whether a country is preponderantly Catholic or Protestant, they often constitute the greater part of any congregation and tend to couple religious and political conservatism.

This statement, however, is too general and simple to be exact. Let me illustrate what I mean. In England and in the United States, the third generation of Catholic Irish immigrants has worked its way up to the middle classes, whereas the first and second generations were laborers, mere proletarians. The same evolution has occurred in the lives of French Canadians. In France the number of those who practice their religion varies broadly

[14] The *J.A.C.* (*Jeunesse Agricole Catholique*).—Tr.

according to the different strata they occupy within the middle classes: very low among some categories of merchants, religious practice rises among others as well as among craftsmen, and is usually highest among persons who work for others, managers and technicians of secondary importance and certain groups of functionaries.

This large bloc of employees and subaltern managers is not peculiar to the Church in France, but can be seen almost everywhere in Western Europe, the United States, Latin America and any complex and industrialized nation. It often seems to hold a monopoly on Catholicism and, because of that very fact and the mysterious psychological laws that govern class relations, it unwittingly drives away its social betters and inferiors.

Today's mass industrialization calls for so many more supervisors and managerial teams, and creates so many more desk jobs, that the middle class in general and the salaried middle class in particular is assuming ever greater importance. Relative independence together with at least a minimum of education and culture enables its members to choose and practice a personal religion more easily. In certain countries at least, the spirit of Catholicism has a happy influence on them and will bear fruit for a long time to come. We should be rash, nevertheless, to imagine that these middle-class groups are naturally religious, naturally Catholic. Similar material causes do not always produce similar effects. The Scandinavian countries are thoroughly middle-class and just as thoroughly de-christianized. Sociological facts are mere conditions, not causes.

*

The practice of religion among the laboring element in industry varies according to place and cultural level. In the Latin nations—like Italy (especially in the North), Spain, France and South-eastern Belgium—it lies far below that of the middle classes and of country people in general. It drops to almost zero in certain suburbs of a megalopolis like Paris or Marseilles, and just about everywhere among the proletariat. Those laborers who practice their religion belong for the most part to the higher strata of the working classes; they have professional training, a trade and, consequently, a measure of personal independence.

In the countries just named, the proletariat seems to think its condition raises an impregnable barrier between the person and religion. The privileged individual who breaks through is considered an exception that only confirms the rule. The misery and perpetual distress of proletarians, their lack of culture and independence, their conformism bred of constant promiscuity at home or

81

at work, the inhumanity of their condition—all these are carriers which spread the disease of religious indifference among them. While Catholics —clergy and faithful—kept looking back to a dead past after the French Revolution, more or less materialistic forms of socialism and, eventually, atheistic communism sought out the proletariat and still hover near it in the Latin countries. Both socialism and communism exerted considerable influence over the leaders of the laboring masses, but their victory is now being counteracted by specialized Catholic Action and the development of Catholic social teaching. Faced with what he saw in his day, Pius XI spoke of "the apostasy of the working class." In the final analysis, the working class never was Catholic: it grew up and became conscious of itself outside of Catholicism.

As I said, our efforts to make up for lost time have been remarkably successful. Still, the few Catholic trade-unions have only a small, though growing, membership. They have hardly touched the proletariat, but do most of their recruiting among skilled laborers, section bosses, functionaries and others who border on the middle classes. Following upon the early but perhaps too swift and spectacular triumphs of the Young Catholic Workers (*J.O.C.*), the Catholic apostolate to the workingman of France and Italy is presently contacting excellent groups which, though active and intrepid, are not numerous enough to improve conditions immediately.

We should, however, note the sharp differences that characterize the spiritual life of workers in various sections of one country. In France, for example, the religious climate changes instantaneously if we go from Paris to Saint-Etienne or from Marseilles to Lille, Roubaix and Tourcoing. So too in Italy when we travel from Piedmont to Venetia. Variations such as these make any general statement imprudent.

We can appreciate how urgently the working classes in those countries need apostolic attention. The Young Catholic Workers movement was founded in Belgium and soon spread to France. The only priest-worker cells in the history of the Church functioned in France and in Southeastern Belgium. Conditions there clamored for just such an experiment, whereas elsewhere it would have been unwarranted, useless or at least premature. Its first stages ended in failure for many reasons— chiefly, perhaps, because of too little preparation and patience and too much publicity. But they have left us inspiring memories of pioneers, like the *abbés* Perrin and Favreau, who died at work. And now new experiments are being planned or conducted: the *Mission ouvrière* in Paris, the *Mission de France*, the efforts of Bishop Ancel, and those of Father Loew in and around Marseilles. "Unless the grain of wheat fall into the ground and die, it remains alone; but if it die, it brings forth much fruit."

At the opposite pole from the Latin countries stand the Germanic and the Anglo-Saxon nations, especially those which have experienced Protestant rule and protection. Alsace and the Flemish part of Belgium were once heterogeneous areas where both conditions existed. A fairly high number of workers practice their religion in Southern Holland, Westphalia, the Rhine Province, Baden and even in Austria. In fact, for the past few years Germany as well as Austria has been witnessing a gradual reconciliation between socialists and those Catholics who are versed in Christian social teaching. Prejudice, distrust, hatred—all are vanishing. Paradoxical though it may seem, the nazi persecution, which oppressed them both, and the threat of ruthless atheistic communism, which provoked the same reaction in them both, have brought them so close that, in Austria, socialists and Catholics work hand in hand to serve the government.

In England, the United States, Australia and New Zealand, Catholicism is striking its roots deep in the lives of workers. Catholics who survived the persecutions have met Irish emigrants in the industrial valley of the Tyne, and as a result the Catholics of England supply the trade-unions and the Labour Party with fighters and leaders. Institutes like the college for Catholic workers at Oxford have trained generations of labor managers. The United States has been progressing along the same path ever since Cardinal Gibbons defended the Knights of Labor in the Roman courts. American workmen unanimously chose Catholic George Meany to head the huge AFL-CIO.

Except for the tiny republic of Costa Rica, South America unfortunately resembles the Latin nations of Europe more than the English-speaking countries just named. Social work and the evangelization of the laboring classes have definitely not kept pace with the progress of city life and administration. As a result, Peronism arose in Argentina and communism has been gathering force in Brazil under the direction of Carlos Prestes. The working classes in these relatively young nations exhibit a warm and demonstrative faith but, lacking discernment, they may easily be lured into various forms of materialism. However, judging by the sound social and apostolic work being done in Chile, Uruguay, Argentina and Brazil, South American Catholics are now alive and alert.

Within the new Christian communities of Africa and Asia, the Faith usually conquers the masses—the poorest, often the most miserable and abandoned. Thus, in India it has won over outcasts, or pariahs, and peasants from still fairly primitive tribes. In general, the aristocracy and what corresponds to our middle classes cling to their traditional paganism or drift into agnosticism and even into the atheism of the West. Occasionally some small but important group or notable individuals—like General and Madame Chiang Kai-shek—will embrace an Anglo-Saxon brand of Protestantism. In colonial districts, the religious fervor of the native converts frequently contrasts with the practical materialism or the conventional, worldly Catholicism of many colonizers. This situation has in the past touched off conflicts between colonial governments and missionaries or local clergymen; and, as we learned in Madagascar and elsewhere, the resultant antagonism does not die with decolonization. When the Mau-Maus revolted against the British authorities in Kenya, many of the Kikuyus who had been condemned to death wanted to die in the Catholic religion. Their wish represents an extreme case, but it also stands as a symbol.

Conditions, however, are not the same everywhere. Catholicism enjoys genuine prestige in the intellectual circles of Japan; in Vietnam, some mandarin families, like the Diems, have recently entered or have been in the Church for several generations; and the conversion of certain African chiefs has prompted that of entire tribes. If space permitted, we could adduce a multitude of other examples.

*

All these analyses underline the infinite sociological variety which today's Catholic communities exhibit according to time, country and culture. They also prove how oversimple, how farfetched and—to put it bluntly—how false is the Marxist view which attacks Catholicism as a "bourgeois phenomenon." The Church's catholicity shines out through her social as well as her geographical multiformity.

It is nevertheless true that countries in the process of industrial development pose religious questions which seem ever present and ever alike. The most serious of them is the dechristianization, not only of the workingman, but of the intellectual and the middle classes. These problems grow apace with the progress of urban civilization and the far-reaching modifications it effects in the structure of society and the psychology of the people. Besides proving that the practice of religion in large cities is higher than in unreligious rural areas but lower than in traditionally religious ones, surveys show that contemporary civilization is not of itself refractory to religion and that Catholicism, though it seems thoroughly rural in

Latin countries, is quite at home in the cities of many Anglo-Saxon nations.

Catholicism is deeply involved in the earth-shaking crisis that has been rocking civilization since the industrial revolution. The brusque transformations forced on humanity open new roads to the Church and obstruct old ones, conceal pitfalls and afford steppingstones. Invariably they present problems, some of which we shall study in the following chapter.

chapter four

The Problems
of
Contemporary Catholicism

At the opening session of the Second World Congress of the Lay Apostolate held in Rome in October of 1957, a tall African Negro, draped in a green garment like a Roman in his toga, uttered in French the first words to be heard at the proceedings: "I give the floor to His Eminence Cardinal Pizzardo."

So simple was the scene that many did not perceive the novelty of it. And yet it summarized and, in a way, solved almost all the major problems confronting contemporary Catholicism—problems like the role of the laity, the missions, the interrelations of religion and culture in a world which is growing closer together, newly formed countries with their material and spiritual needs, ways of presenting Christianity to non-European peoples, international relations within the Church, the hierarchy and the interaction of the spiritual and the temporal, the personal and the group attitude of Catholics in a technical and urban civilization whose improved transportation and communications facilitate international gatherings.

These are some of the questions, listed without respect to the order in which we shall study them. Some, like the last, are new. Others, though stated in modern terms, are as old as the Church herself and sometimes as ancient as the Chosen People and Abraham, their father.

*

The first and perhaps most pressing problem is that of weaving the Church into the very fabric, structure, mentality and mores of our brand-new civilization—a mass urban and technological civilization, which only yesterday was graphic, controlled by books and newspapers, and today is increasingly audio-visual, shaped by radio, television and motion pictures. As an organism, the Church must implant herself in time if she is to survive; but, as a guide to eternity, she cannot be identified with or linked to transience. Despite what some Catholics think, she must follow the inviolable law of incarnation and throw out roots into the world.

Tardiness and reluctance to obey that law account, to some extent, for the waning interest, the wavering faith and the utter dechristianization we see all about us. Historical investigations into the decline of religion in large cities reveal numerous causes, some constant, most of them varying with

92

time and place; but they usually pinpoint a few basic reasons: namely, the hesitation of churches and clergymen to follow the double progress of demography and urbanization, and the slowness of priests and faithful to adapt themselves to the sociological and psychological changes wrought by the growth of our modern cities. Paris and Marseilles bear witness to the decisive role these factors play in the areligious or irreligious comportment of the laboring classes. The uprooted who hastened to answer factory whistles found, in their shabby neighborhood, neither priests nor churches enough to receive them; and the clergy, cut off as they were, knew nothing of the psychology or even the living conditions of the working classes. The specifically urban quality of Anglo-Saxon Catholicism proves our point.

In many lands, religion, which had originated in the cities in apostolic times, formed noble and poetic ties with the earth and the seasons, the peasantry and its toil. The Ember Day liturgy still alludes to them and stirs the hearts of city dwellers who remember their farm background. Regrettably but unavoidably, the urban revolution severed those bonds; and, as a result, many nostalgic Catholics clung desperately to gilded memories of their rustic past.

Something of their attitude persists among not a few Catholics—intellectuals mostly—who look down their nose at technology, despise the newest media for thought dissemination and, while using all its conveniences, consider contemporary civilization foredoomed to damnation, a *massa damnata,* a soulless world. They would do better to see it as a world searching, as Bergson said, for a "supplement to its soul." Their view, however, is not wholly unfounded: some of their fear and antipathy is legitimate and would become stupid only if erected into a systematic hatred of all things modern. We may prefer to have been born in the thirteenth rather than in the twentieth century, but that does not matter. The question is: Should we who live in the 1960's live in the manner of the 1960's—except, of course, for sin—using for God's glory the resources of the 1960's? The innumerable lights of a city can proclaim His glory as well as the meteors in the sky, the phosphorescent creatures on the crest of the waves or the glowworm by the side of the road.

There is surely something extreme, paroxysmal, about civilization today. We see it in the United States, where the young are confused and disenchanted for having been given too much too soon and robbed of dreams for the future. We see it also—infinitely more dangerous—in Russia, where so many have been dehumanized by industrial, utilitarian and atheistic communism. At the same time, we cannot forget that the United States is actually experiencing a religious revival that bespeaks unquenched thirst deep in the soul. For all its persecutions and technical triumphs, the Supreme Soviet has not extirpated religion from the hearts of the Russian people. Some proponents of modern civilization may seem barbarians who smell of machine oil, but let us remember that the Church once baptized others who smelled of the forest. Why should she fail to communicate grace to the barbarians of this day and age?

We are living in the era of Luniks and Sputniks, atomic energy, automation, cybernetics, and incredible advances in biology and experimental psychology—mixed blessings, no doubt, fraught with danger as well as opportunity, but all of which we must humanize and divinize, accepting them because they belong to the time in which God has placed us so that we may render an account of them in eternity.

We are still far from that ideal. How many priests can converse with intellectuals trained in the sciences, or even mere technicians? How many can effectively use radio and television to preach the word of God from the housetops? Some Catholic laymen in the motion picture industry turn out "pious" movies—a fairly easy matter and always good box office; but how many can produce films that are imbued with the spirit of Catholicism, films that treat of human problems with a specifically Christian outlook? Suppose we check our parishes, our societies, our charitable organizations. Are they suited to the requirements of city life? How can we reach the underprivileged who live in the promiscuity of shacks or workingmen's hovels? Or how enter the tidy apartments of the middle classes, snugly wrapped up in their comfort and their precious little individualism?

If we really want to answer those questions, we just have to look at our Church architecture. In the name of tradition, we have clung to outmoded ways of thinking and building; for too long we have ignored both the needs arising from and the possibilities offered by the context of city life. Encouraged by the brothers Perret, however, architects like Novarina, Baur and Le Corbusier are boldly creating new designs and effecting a change which is most perceptible in Switzerland and in Southern Germany.

Other points we might look into are our vocabulary, which, failing to change with changing situations, has grown incomprehensible to our contemporaries; our liturgical language—Latin—further and further removed from modern vernaculars, less and less indispensable for culture; that culture itself, bound up with a tradition of Greco-Roman humanism that is increasingly remote from this scientific and technological age; and, lastly, the constant symbolism of our liturgy in a world which has forgotten how to read symbols and crams all its knowledge into abbreviations and algebraic formulae. The list could run on almost indefinitely.

Only the irresponsible would conclude that we should jettison our priceless heritage to adapt ourselves to the modern world, as only the obtuse would minimize the manifold problems caused by the conflict between past and present.

It affords but small consolation to say that this conflict is temporary and that everything will come out right in the end if only we wait patiently and passively. Present social structures and viewpoints will be altered, of course; and we can hope that human nature, disoriented by too drastic a change in civilization, will regain its equilibrium by making the right choices and correcting its scale of values. For example, jazz and rock 'n' roll will die long before the immemorial practice of taxation. Yet we should wait in vain for some wheel to turn full circle and deposit us right in the middle of the rural past. More than that, we must realize that the general trend nowadays is to sweep away the small peasant groups that still exist in parts of Africa, Asia and even in certain sectors of industrialized zones. We should be foolish, too, if we expected the needed choices and readjustments to be made automatically, from the sheer force of necessity. City life, for instance, is always and everywhere blighted by alcoholism, drug addiction

97

and sexual laxity; and only a half-witted optimist could believe that men would spontaneously give up these evils in disgust. The masses will be capable of free choice only when they have been strengthened by the spirit. Now, Catholicism communicates that spirit; but Catholicism can work in our day only if it is actual and effective—in other words, adapted to present needs, just as in the past it was adapted to older cultures and civilizations.

This efficacious presence of the Church in the world is the goal of countless experiments being conducted under the guidance of the hierarchy by Catholics all over the globe, in the suburbs of Paris and London and Chicago, in television and motion picture studios, in laboratories and research centers, in the work of Sonnenschein in Berlin or *abbé* Pierre in Paris or Father Pire throughout Europe.

*

The race between the Catholic Faith and unbelief since the turn of the century makes our task all the more urgent. Neutral and indefinite, the term *unbelief* should fool no one. It can mean many different things; but right now it means an out-and-out rejection not only of Catholicism but of Christianity and any form of religion, a refusal to believe in every spiritual reality that transcends man.

98

From this point of view, our era is vastly different from earlier ones. Until the eighteenth century, Catholicism encountered obstacles and opposition from other religious groups, which did or did not constitute distinct Churches. Among them were Islamism in the Middle Ages; Catharism, a recrudescence of Manichaeanism that tried to subvert the Church from within; the so-called Orthodox Churches of the Orient; countless heresies and, especially, Protestantism. During the nineteenth century, Catholicism had to battle foes that could not properly be called religious. Its enemies —rationalism, liberalism and secularism—funneled into Freemasonry, which often became anti-Church, especially in Latin nations. But they denied only part of the truth. Disputing certain aspects of dogma or even dogma as a whole, they did not attack morality (at least in its essentials), the notion of objective truth or, often, belief in God and the soul.

Not so in the twentieth century. The Church today faces three powerful adversaries who oppose her on every point. The first, positivism of a more or less scientific and definitely secular variety, seeks to create a world sufficient unto itself and refuses to consider not only religious questions but any philosophical problem which transcends the logic of science. The second, atheistic communism, not content with persecuting every type of religious

99

life, denies in practice the existence of objective truth and morality. The third, godless existentialism, finds morbid delight in despair and insists that man and the world are fundamentally absurd. Despite differences of degree and open contradictions, these three tendencies agree on one point: they all reject and repudiate *a priori* and totally, beforehand and without exception, every form of religion and spiritual metaphysics.

Even those of our contemporaries who do not subscribe to these ideas but explicitly disclaim them—even they are influenced. Positivism rubs off on certain Catholics. For proof, let the French recall the sorry episode of *L'Action française,* and let all of us observe the conduct of skilled workers, businessmen and savants who call themselves Catholics. Atheistic communism contaminates the thinking of others, especially those who like to call themselves "progressives" whether they are or not. Others again, by their reasoning and behavior, prove that they practice the "situational morality" of existentialism.

The apologetics and the catechesis of yesterday are inadequate to these new attacks. Of course, the battles of the distant or recent past are not over: controversy still rages between Catholics and Protestants, Christians and liberals, believers and rationalists; there remain Moslems, occultists and deists to be catechized and brought into the Church. In this respect, nothing has changed. But the arguments and the approaches that convince them hardly move the positivist disciples of Jean Rostand, the racist followers of Adolf Hitler, the communistic heirs of Lenin, the existentialist pupils of Heidegger and Sartre, or even the simple and decent unbeliever who reads Albert Camus and Ernest Hemingway.

We Catholics, therefore, must do much thinking, whether our individual forte be research, theory or action. It would be pointless to pursue adversaries who no longer exist. It would be most dangerous to boast of adaptation and proceed to twist the truth, as the modernists and the progressives do; or invoke doctrinal intransigence and refuse to adapt ourselves to present-day needs, as the integralists do. And, finally, it would be disastrous to think that Catholicism, because it must combat communism, might be defined as a sort of anti-communism; for thus we would drag the Faith down to the level of its opponents and fall into the McCarthyism which attracts too many Catholics and Protestants alike and plays right into the hands of the communists.

One example will illustrate both the way to proceed and the difficulty of doing so. The teaching of Sigmund Freud dominates our century. Now,

101

truth to tell, that teaching is extremely question-able. As a combination doctor and philosopher, Freud discovered facts which laid the foundation for depth psychology; he devised a clinical technique which has been known to cure certain mental ills; he proffered scientific explanations, some of which were valid finds, some almost worthless, and some mere labels that explained nothing; and he evolved a metaphysical system that is positivistic, pansexual and a-Christian if not anti-Christian. Direct or indirect, his influence can be sensed in the everyday use of terms like *complex* and *repression*. Some Catholics have rejected Freudianism altogether; some have embraced it to the detriment of their faith and common sense; but some—patient, perspicacious men like Dalbiez, Nodet and Karl Stern—have studied the facts and separated truth from falsehood, thereby showing us what we must do with any doctrine in any realm of thought.

We may, for instance, disagree with the theories of scholar-philosopher-poet Teilhard de Chardin (I personally think some of them highly debatable); but we may not doubt the sublimity, the scope and the timeliness of his work, or the prestige it enjoys among so many of our contemporaries, Christian and non-Christian alike, precisely because it incorporates into a Catholic synthesis the concept of evolution, which many once considered contrary to Christian teaching. We may deem his synthesis premature and his arguments inconclusive; but this we must admit: they point the way for future investigation.

*

The Church's willingness to adapt herself to a changing world attests to the missionary spirit which animates her today. She is perhaps even more of a missionary now than in the glorious periods of her history: principally, she is more intensely mission-minded in all her members and in all her activities. But her missionary desires expose her to new problems or at least to old ones in modern dress.

The missionary fervor of Catholics has been kindled by their growing awareness that the Church is a minority group in today's world. With certain demographic and geographic forces threatening the object of their faith and love, they realize that their one weapon is an increase of missionary work. And they understand that the concept of missionary work must be broadened to include not only the specialized activity of missioners in Islam or pagan lands but the whole apostolate of the Church, even in Christian countries.

With regard to missions in the classical sense of the word, we can rejoice over the immense progress in theory and technique effected under the inspiration of theologians and scholars, like Fathers Schmidt, Charles and Tempels, *abbé* Schmid-

lin, Dom Neut and Doctor H. C. E. Zacharias;
men of action, like Father Lebbe and Bishop de
Guébriant; or others, like Father Aupiais, who
have combined scientific study with actual missionary work. We must salute Belgium, the home
of two leading centers of missionary thought:
Saint-André's Abbey at Lophem-les-Bruges and
the Jesuit Studium at Louvain. The period between both World Wars purged missiology of any
romantic sentimentality that was vitiating it, re-
affirmed the essential objectives of missionary work
and raised it far above petty nationalism and imperialism. Papal documents from the *Rerum Ec-
clesiae* of Benedict XV to the *Fidei donum* of Pius
XII serve as both milestones and guideposts along
this road of intellectual progress. A quick way to
measure the ground covered is to compare the
missionary magazines published after the first
World War with those published after the second.

Thus enlightened and purified, missionary ac-
tivity goes on. Of necessity, it is becoming ever
more international. Blessed with a true vocation,
France is still a prominent worker, thanks to
priestly groups like the *Missions étrangères* of
Paris and the *Missions africaines* of Lyons. But
Belgium, the United States with the Maryknoll
Fathers, Germany, England, Canada, Holland and
Ireland labor at her side in the field afar. Simi-
larly, the Society for the Propagation of the Faith,

though founded in France, has spread throughout the world.

Peculiar to our times is the active part played by the laity in missionary work. Some, as in Belgium's *A.U.C.A.M.*, support the program of evangelization in Christian countries, whereas others, as in France's *Société des Auxiliaires des missions* and *Ad Lucem* with its counterparts the world over, engage in activities more directly connected with the missions.

Missions are not an end in themselves: their whole purpose is to establish local Churches which will be wholly indigenous and self-governing within Catholicism. The nineteenth century seemed to have lost sight of that goal; but the twentieth has fully rediscovered it, especially since the naming of the first Chinese and Japanese bishops by Pope Pius XI. Now every continent, race and civilization has its own priests and bishops. And that is only the beginning.[1] Europeans who identified the Church with Western civilization misunderstood this reaffirmation of missionary

[1] Dr. Folliet's assertion is borne out by the fact that on May 8, 1960, His Holiness Pope John XXIII consecrated fourteen missionary bishops, among whom were an Australian, a Japanese and eight Africans. The year before, he consecrated other African bishops, established seven apostolic prefectures in the Congo alone, appointed John Kodwo Amissah the first Negro Archbishop of Ghana, and gave Africa her first Negro prince of the Church in the person of His Eminence Laurian Cardinal Rugambwa, Bishop of Rutabo, Tanganyika.—Tr.

goals and combatted this insistence on the Church's universality, but for the last few years their resistance has been but the force of inertia. Nothing can keep the Church from being catholic.

But these are difficult times. Today's missionaries labor in a period of transition. Some of the changes occur gradually, almost imperceptibly; others are sudden and violent. Colonization is yielding to self-government. Almost everywhere, an upsurge of national feeling—with occasional racist overtones—is stirring colonies that were recently liberated, turning them against Europe and even against the white race and Western culture. Other peoples are clamoring for freedom. Underdeveloped areas are fighting for survival. And just as, in the past, the Church was involved in the great discoveries and subsequent colonization, so now she is involved in all this turmoil. She must not only recognize but sanction the legitimate claims of Asian and African peoples. She must temper their resentment, calm their ill-feelings and purify their exaggerated patriotism, lest it degenerate into nationalism or some new form of imperialism. She must also encourage technical and economic progress, insist on social justice and arm backward groups against the allurements and dangers of communism. Indeed, atheistic communism has already invaded some mission fields and sown them with the blood of martyrs. The mere possibility of its spreading to all underde-

veloped nations should make us understand the
privilege and the grave duty we have of training
native laymen to discharge their responsibilities in
the social and national life of their countries. Let
us look at Africa, war-torn in the North and hate-
ridden in the South. As we observe the Church living, laboring and suffering there in the midst of
political dissatisfaction and racial violence, we can
form some idea of the difficulties that beset today's
missioners.

Less immediate but no less critical are the problems created when different cultures and civilizations cross paths. At such a time, newly formed or
reorganized nations experience contradictory feelings, wanting on the one hand to absorb the Western culture necessary for their development and
wishing on the other to remain faithful to the
traditions and characteristics of their own culture.
Now, although the very nature of the Church pre-
cludes her being linked to any one civilization or
type of culture, historically she appears to non-
Europeans as essentially bound up with the West.
Consequently, since her relations with any country
or culture are historical and, therefore, contingent
and accidental, she must strive to free her fundamental self from whatever elements in those relations would seem to impugn her universality.
Harmless and obvious as it seems, that statement
presupposes a heroic program of work, study and
abnegation.

Here again the religious art and architecture of mission lands could serve as a test. Retaining regional, folkloric archaism would be a mistake—almost as serious as importing Western traditions indiscriminately. At present, psychological truth consists in steering clear of two extremes: the view that confuses Christianity with Western culture, and the unthinking retention of obsolete cultures. The first attitude is shortsighted, the second betokens ethnological estheticism rather than the true missionary spirit.

If the missionary ideals of our day could be embodied in one man, I would suggest that that man was *abbé* Jules Monchanin, a brilliant young priest from Lyons who went to India, offered his services to a native bishop and became a perfect native himself so that he could live with the Indians, heroically adapting himself to their way of life till fatigue and privation led to his premature death. Silent though he was, he eloquently proclaimed the spirit of an epoch.

*

The Church's missionary zeal likewise governs her relations with our separated brethren, whether Orthodox or Protestant, and with the Jews, our ancestors in the worship of God. We can only rejoice at the progress made in those relations of late.

First, with regard to the Jews. Although anti-Semitism still poisons the minds of some Catholics,

108

it has been totally purged from the best. That was evident during Hitler's persecution, when the hunted Jews found Catholics—hierarchy, clergy and faithful—to be their most courageous and helpful protectors. Anti-Semitism is now the property of those whose faith is weak and unenlightened or of those who have no faith and therefore lean toward Hitlerism, fascism or Stalinism. At the same time, Jews as a whole are drawing closer to Catholicism, and some are entering the Church— well-known figures like Raïssa Maritain, Henri Bergson, Karl Stern, Edith Stein, Max Jacob and Rabbi Zolli. In Israel herself a small group of Zionist Jews who have become Christians bear witness to Christ among His own people.

Catholic-Protestant relations are constantly improving. Almost purely "political" at one time, they are becoming more and more spiritual. Certain tensions persist, naturally, ranging from antagonism to opposition and misunderstanding, as in Spain, several Latin American nations, Ulster, parts of the United States and Canada and, as evidenced not too long ago, a few cities in England. Still, in most Occidental countries the situation has completely changed from a hundred years ago. A look at modern Germany, for example, makes Bismarck's Kulturkampf seem like something from ancient history.

Some Protestant groups are growing closer to Catholicism, notably among German and Scandi-

navian Lutherans and among adherents of England's High Church (which, incidentally, calls herself Anglo-Catholic rather than Protestant). As a
result, individuals and sometimes whole communities have been converted. Thus Anglicanism has
given the Roman Catholic Church in England
some of her ablest theologians, from John Henry
Cardinal Newman to Monsignor Ronald Knox.
The desire to draw nearer is producing happy results even among the Calvinists, as we can see in
the Protestant monastic community at Taizé.

The spirit of unity, of ecumenism, is gradually
dispelling the spirit of rivalry and competition.
Under the inspiration of men like Lord Halifax in
England, Oscar Cullmann in Germany, and Cardinal Mercier and the *abbés* Portal and Couturier
in France, Anglo-Catholics, Protestants and Roman Catholics are examining their mutual rela-
tionships with patience, charity and strict regard
for the truth. Unity cannot, of course, be achieved
in a trice: there are too many obstacles to be over-
come, too many conditions to be fulfilled; but we
do see evidence of a burning desire to reunite the
Churches as soon as possible.

Relations between Catholicism and the Orthodox Churches are rendered more difficult by the
fact that most of them lie behind the Iron Curtain
and are either persecuted by atheistic communism
or used by it for anti-Roman propaganda. When

free, they are improving their relations with Rome. The most active Orthodox groups in Greece and the Near East study our Catholic Action techniques. In Nestorian Abyssinia, Emperor Haile Selassie has entrusted the University of Addis Ababa to religious from Canada. And in India, ancient Syro-Malabar communities are returning to the Church of Rome.

There is no doubt that these spiritual odysseys depend in part on material conditions. The Church has little to fear from Protestantism, since it is torn by division and sapped by the indifferentism bequeathed it by the liberals; neither are the Orthodox Churches much of a threat, since they often live on the memory of a glorious past and are too nationalistic to become apostles to the world. Divided Christendom, furthermore, sees the stupidity of wasting its strength on petty contests when confronted by common enemies like nazism and communism.

I have spoken of *conditions,* and that is the right word—not *causes.* Conditions remove obstacles and dispel prejudice; they facilitate a return to the Church, but the return itself is caused by something deeper, something in one's very soul. The return of our separated brethren poses all kinds of problems: matters of theology and Canon Law, and questions of psychology and sociology. Utter intransigence was relatively easier than the task

111

we now face of conciliating the claims of truth and charity, unity and legitimate diversity.

*

But the missionary spirit does not stop there. It must win back to Christ and His Church those who have abandoned their religion for indifference or hostile unbelief.

In today's world, "mission lands" lie just beyond our garden gate. Without exaggerating the extent of dechristianization and without branding heathen those areas where the practice of religion has merely dropped off, we must face the facts courageously. If we do, we will observe that, in countries which have been Catholic from of old, indifference is paralyzing sectors that are clearly delimitable for either geographic or sociological reasons. And we will have to conclude that such sectors need genuine missionary work as badly as pagan lands. We are asked, not to maintain or even defend the Faith there, but rather to re-establish or really establish it for the first time. This is so in Latin countries, where the working classes by and large exist outside the Church and are proselytized by anticlerical socialists or atheistic communists. Anglo-Saxon nations fare no better, for, there, oppidans and country people have turned from Protestantism to paganism. Even Catholic lands like Ireland and French-speaking Canada afford scope to the missionary spirit, since their external religiosity often conceals indifference.

Accordingly, the missionary spirit works throughout the Catholic Church, making greater gains and lesser in different countries and regions, in different sectors of large cities and in different milieux. The inevitable diversity of conditions, needs, activities and soul states presents a major problem to the Church, which must always remain one and indivisible and march steadily toward the future and eternity. But in the final analysis, her missionary zeal derives from life itself and the breath of the Holy Spirit.

Our parishes are once again becoming missional. From France—where it began with Father Chevrier and pastors like *abbés* Remillieux and Michonneau, who formed workingmen's parishes—the idea of parish renewal is traveling around the world, as witness the many translations of *abbé* Michonneau's writings.[2] A parish's missionary activity shows forth in liturgical ceremonies and pastoral dealings, and occasionally in works of charity. Here and there throughout Christendom we find

[2] The Newman Press has published translations of three books by *abbé* Michonneau: *Revolution in a City Parish,* with a Foreword by Cardinal Cushing (1949); *The Missionary Spirit in Parish Life* (1952, out of print); and *Catholic Action in the Parish* (1955, out of print).—Tr.

pioneer parishes; and, though many are content to follow at a distance, the general movement is forward.

Missionary enthusiasm is also energizing the many branches of Catholic Action. These branches vary considerably from one country to another, and in old ones like France their ramifications become so complex as to bewilder all but the initiate. General Catholic Action groups all social classes into vast organizations; specialized Catholic Action adapts itself to the milieux in which it functions; and movements like the Legion of Mary, the Christophers and the Sword of the Spirit are animated by a spirituality of their own. None of these organizations is satisfied merely to maintain what has already been established; each, instead, is determined to gain ground and, to that end, has set itself specific objectives and means. Some progress faster than others, some languish and die; but in general all are striving to conquer their part of the world for Christ.

At this point, it is appropriate to recall how fast the Young Catholic Workers movement developed into a world-wide organization. Founded in Belgium a little over thirty years ago, this prototype of specialized Catholic Action soon fanned out over the whole world and, in 1957, displayed its vitality on the occasion of an international pilgrimage to Rome.

It is missionary ardor, finally, which imbues countless associations working outside the framework of the parish and of formal Catholic Action. Among them are religious congregations like the Little Brothers and the Little Sisters of Jesus; the *Scalabrini,* who minister to Italian emigrants; the *Frères missionnaires,* who announce the Gospel in country districts; secular institutes of every kind; and homes for working girls. The inventory could go on indefinitely and still be incomplete, since new groups are constantly springing up with amazing vitality.

But wherever he labors, the missioner will inevitably encounter obstacles and difficulties. Gaps between classes, countries and cultures create tensions and sometimes lead to hostility and permanent division. Contacting and filtering into new milieux necessitates innovations and adjustments which are painful and at times tragic, as in the case of France's priest-workers. Consider the hordes of workingmen in Latin countries who have strayed from Catholicism to Marxism and live, collectivized and isolated, like strangers among their own people. Evangelizing them is as difficult as it is imperative, for how shall we adapt ourselves to them perfectly without compromising our catholicity, which should be not only international and supranational but social and suprasocial? Of the answers suggested so far, none has been complete, none proof against failure.

*

Not by usurpation or main force but rather in generous response to the Church's own request, laymen—or the laity, to use the current term—occupy an increasingly important place in her apostolic and missionary program. This she has willed, not solely to remedy the shortage of priests and religious, but to meet the needs of this indifferent or unbelieving generation, which, as a rule, she can reach only through laymen who witness to Christ in their respective circles. Her understanding of the situation and her solicitude gave birth to Catholic Action and have nourished its wondrous growth since the days between both World Wars.

Laymen, as we know, have always been active in the Church; but perhaps never before have they served in such numbers, acted with such authority or been so conscious of their role as God's Chosen People in the Church. Catholic social activity has shown them their temporal responsibilities as Christians living in the world; Catholic Action, their responsibilities as apostles who share in the work of the hierarchy; and the missionary revival, their responsibilities as subjects of God's kingdom, with regard to the interior life of the community, its worship, its liturgy and the preaching of the word. They understand that they are the arms and the muscles of the Church as she labors to extend her reign; and they sense that they afford a glimpse

116

of her face, her heart and even her mind insofar as they each contribute to the flowering of Catholic thought in the normal evolution of public opinion within the Church.

This awakening of the laity is one more cause for joy. In speaking of the phenomenon, I do not much care for terms like *promotion* and *majority,* which awkwardly try to describe a spiritual reality in legal parlance. The laity has not been promoted: it has become conscious of its mission. It has not attained its majority: it has, rather, comprehended the duties incumbent on any mature Catholic freed from slavery by baptism, strengthened by confirmation and nourished by the Eucharist. Was it by chance that the laity took a new lease on Catholic life as soon as Saint Pius X advocated frequent communion for all?

No eclogue this awakening, but a very serious matter. Our contemporaries speak of "awareness," and we know that their awareness is sometimes—indeed, often—tantamount to a crisis in the realm of conscience; for, the more genuinely Christian and Catholic they become, the more critical and exacting they are with regard not only to themselves but to the other faithful, the clergy and the hierarchy. They cannot brook imperfection or routine and often censure shortcomings with excessive and somewhat naïve impatience. Because they themselves give so much—give everything, in fact—they expect still more from those who urged such generosity on them in the first place. What they forget is that their standards are hard to meet, especially in areas where the clergy suffers from faulty training or lack of vocations.

As Saint Francis de Sales reminds us, wherever we find humans we also find human nature—that is, weakness and sin. Some laymen think themselves adults though only adolescents or even children. In their immaturity, they are content to protest and dream but refuse to put their shoulder to the wheel like responsible workers. Impatient and intransigent, others turn bitter, defiant; they develop a curious sort of anticlericalism and, having little use for priests, would like to laicize everything. Certain types fancy themselves Prophets, Doctors and Fathers of the Church—or, worse yet, Mothers of the Church. A few become clericalists and, for having lost sight of their true vocation, seem rather like would-be priests or religious.

Our revitalized laity needs training, guidance and support, all of which are easier to discuss than to provide. Because of its immense and somewhat undisciplined strength, I sometimes liken the laity to a tame lion. If it must be drugged into submission, it ought never to have been awakened at all; if it must always be fettered, it will never test its strength; but if it is allowed to run uncontrolled,

God alone knows what damage it can do, even with the best of intentions.

Fortunately, the Church today is firmly established on a unified and well-organized hierarchy. The days of major schisms and heresies seem past. In fact, since the nineteenth century, most dissidents have vanished, leaving behind them only a few coteries or ephemeral sects. The danger nowadays is the defection of individual Catholics and gradual leakage from the Church. Yet, strong and solid, she can trust her lay apostles to prevent loss and bring the straying sheep back to their Shepherd.

*

Laymen are bound up with matters temporal—the family, work, government and culture—and for all these they are responsible before God. Through their instrumentality, the Church can become incarnate and infuse into the temporal her spirit of divine love and brotherhood under our common Father.

In ages past, her incarnation was effected against other backgrounds and by very different means. The feudal system, the communal movement, absolute monarchy—all served successively, yet none ever seemed the only or even the best context for the Church's message. It is true that after the

119

French Revolution Catholicism was momentarily nonplused, torn between nostalgia for the old regime and the glittering promises of the new. For a time, liberals and conservatives filled the air with their disputes. Then—say, about 1830—the Church began to speak to the world again through two organizations that have been evolving slowly: the Catholic Social Movement and the Christian Democratic Movement.

From being identified with the same groups (like that around *L'Avenir*) or the same persons (like Frédéric Ozanam), these two tendencies have often been considered one, whereas, despite kinship and similarities, they are distinct and sometimes even opposed to one another. In the register of the Catholic Social Movement we find such names as Albert de Mun, la Tour du Pin, Léon Harmel, Marius Gonin and Eugène Duthoit in France; Ketteler and Kolping in Germany; Toniolo in Italy; Vogelsang in Austria; Mermillod, Decurtins and Montenach in Switzerland; Manning in England; Verhaegen in Belgium; and many others. In that of the Christian Democrats we see Windthorst and Brüning in Germany; Don Sturzo and Filippo Meda in Italy; Pottier and Carton de Wiart in Belgium; Etienne Lamy, Marc Sangier and Robert Cornilleau in France; and Lord Acton in England. There should be a third register for persons who do not fit into either category—men

120

like the great nineteenth-century American prel-
ates Cardinal Gibbons and Archbishop Ireland.

Opposed by anticlerical and Catholic liberals
alike, by socialists and conservative Catholics, both
movements nevertheless succeeded and won the
Church's official approval. Papal encyclicals like
the *Rerum novarum* of Leo XIII and the *Quadra-
gesimo anno* of Pius XI as well as the messages of
Pius XII sanctioned the success of the Catholic
Social Movement. Although the pronouncement
of Pius XII on the Christian concept of democracy
did not bestow the same unqualified approbation
on the Christian Democrats, it recognized their
attitude as legitimate and oriented it resolutely
toward the sort of future envisioned by the Church.

And now, having passed the test of time, the
Catholic Social Movement is gaining ground the
world over. It comprises very diverse organisms—
some, like the *Semaines sociales,* directly related
to the Church; and others, like the Catholic trade-
unions, merely inspired by her teachings. It does
not bear as much fruit in some countries as in
others—especially those deprived of political freedom—but it is implanted in almost all. (How
heartwarming to see that the *Semaines sociales,*
begun in France about 1904, are now held in more
than twenty countries, and most recently in Japan
and in the English-speaking part of Canada!)

121

Neither has the Catholic Social Movement penetrated equally far into every class. Employers, in general, are far less amenable to it than others, and it is noticeable that they have not yet organized along Christian lines. Still, the movement has had some influence on every class and group. That it is strong and productive appears from the fruit it has borne far and wide: in France, the *Semaines sociales,* Catholic trade-unions and countless social services, foremost among which is *le Secours catholique;* in Belgium, the *Boerenbond,* which bands farmers together for mutual aid; in Germany, the *Gesellen-Verein* or the *Kolping-Haüse* for apprentices; in Italy, the *A.C.L.I.* with its message for the workingman; in the United States, the Catholic Worker's shelter for the poor and the Friendship Houses for better relations between whites and Negroes; in Canada, the co-operative societies of Antigonish and the credit-unions established by Desjardins; in the United States, England, Australia and New Zealand, the very presence of Catholics in union organizations; and, lastly, international societies like the one founded to protect young girls away from home.

The Catholic Social Movement has this advantage, that it combines solid doctrine with extreme flexibility. Its doctrine is based on the Church's social teaching; its flexibility shuns methodism and academicism to facilitate and speed the process of adaptation. Because of its perpetual and almost imperceptible evolution, the movement has survived both World Wars and successfully transplanted itself from the liberal, capitalistic, individualistic and democratic world of yesterday to the organizational, collective, authoritarian and even totalitarian world of today. Granted that the adaptation is not complete and that some branches have withered and died, yet it seems certain that the Catholic Social Movement will thrive for the time being.

The state of the Christian Democratic Movement, on the contrary, does not warrant quite as much optimism. Long combated and oppressed (as in fascist Italy and nazi Germany) or kept in second place and given only a supporting role (as in France until the war of 1939), the Christian Democratic Movement emerged after World War II as a force that was ancient, tested, already traditional and nevertheless new. The Popular Republican Movement tasted but a brief triumph in France. But in Italy and Germany, the Christian Democrats produced two distinguished statesmen, Alcide de Gasperi and Konrad Adenauer, who started from zero and, by the most peaceful and democratic means, admirably restored their respective countries. Their achievements will live in history and, alone, would justify the past performance of the Christian Democratic Movement.

Austria's socialists and Christian Democrats have wisely forgotten their differences to work together for their material and cultural betterment. Perhaps their most splendid accomplishment is the miraculous rebirth of Austrian patriotism. The Christian concept of democracy long held sway in Costa Rica, one of the few peaceful and stable countries in Latin America.

And yet on almost every front the Christian Democratic Movement shows signs of weakening. For one thing, having originated in the days of liberalism and parliamentary democracy, it has not always adjusted satisfactorily to the new conditions created by the progress of technology and the acceleration of history. For another, the existence of Catholic parties that parade as such and solicit the votes of Catholics may afford certain advantages to the Church; but it places her in the unfortunate position of seeming involved in politics and enmeshed in temporalities, and further causes uneasiness among the parties themselves (for they often go their separate ways) and among rightist or leftist Catholics who disagree with them.

The Christian Democratic Movement, moreover, is not the sole means of effecting agreement and collaboration between the spiritual and the temporal. In English-speaking nations, for example, not all Catholics belong to the same party:

124

most of those in England seem to support the Labour Party, but others are Conservative; many Catholic families in the United States traditionally favor the Democrats, but the Republicans also boast Catholic voters, campaigners and leaders. France's Catholics are unevenly divided among all the parties, from the extreme right to the socialist left; but the largest and most coherent group belongs to the Popular Republican Movement. The Catholics of semi-totalitarian Poland are trying to work their way into their country's political life. Latin America offers the greatest variety of political conditions, including liberal democracy in Uruguay and Trujillo's dictatorship in San Domingo; yet, as demonstrated in Argentina and Venezuela, it appears that Catholics throughout the continent are increasingly opposed to dictatorial forms of government. In the young countries of Asia and Africa, some Catholics support authoritarian governments like that of Diem in Vietnam, while others establish "Catholic parties" mostly along the lines of the Christian Democratic Movement and others join that neutral party which seems most sympathetic to Christianity and most inclined to further their interests.

These variations, these complexities, these divergences, all prove that a Catholic party of the Christian Democratic variety is not a universally satisfactory solution in space. Whether it is more

125

so in time—even for nations where Christian democracy has performed brilliantly—only the future, and doubtlessly the near future, will tell.

*

The present is already answering another question that embraces the spiritual and the temporal: How must the Church acquit herself in a world that is becoming international and unified?

In a way, the Church has always had an answer for it, since, being supranational by nature, she is also international in fact. According to Cardinal Feltin's nice distinction, she has always practiced "vertical catholicity," so that all Catholic activity occurring anywhere on earth meets and co-ordinates at the very center of Catholicism, the Rome of the popes. This vertical catholicity is all the more real in our day, when better communications allow of more and speedier contacts and so facilitate centralization on the national as well as the international level. Increasing centralization, however, raises certain practical problems, such as the congestion of the central organisms by a rush of requests and petitions, or the co-ordination of local enterprises and duties with those of the central directing bureau. The age of Gallicanism and Febronianism is clearly past, but that does not mean we shall never have problems again.

For a long time, vertical internationalization sufficed to ensure the Church's catholicity. Far removed from one another by provincial particularities and restricted communications, local Catholic communities nevertheless shared, with regard to Rome, a common allegiance which guaranteed their unity and their participation in the Christian spirit of universality. Today, with the shrinking globe and the quickening pace of international life, vertical catholicity is more indispensable than ever before; but, to return to Cardinal Feltin's felicitous distinction, it must be supplemented and complemented by horizontal catholicity—that is, by direct contact and co-operation between Christians all over the world, whether on a national, international or universal level.

For the sake of illustration, let us consider how necessary it is to co-ordinate efforts made to guarantee the spiritual life of immigrants throughout the world, how desirable and useful to have Catholics serving in international agencies like the *C.E.C.A.* or the European Assembly, or in worldwide ones like the United Nations Conference on International Organization (UNCIO), the Food and Agriculture Organization (FAO), the World Health Organization (WHO) and the United Nations Educational, Scientific and Cultural Organization (UNESCO). No wonder Catholics are founding many international societies—so many, in fact, that there is need of a special one (the Office of Catholic International Societies) to serve as a common denominator for the rest. This global

127

growth is probably one of the most characteristic features of our age.

Well may we feel happy and proud to see the Church not merely follow but precede and guide mankind along the road to world unity. But this road, too, is fissured, bordered by swamps and paved with obstacles. In theory, there should be no conflict between the exigencies of vertical catholicity and those of horizontal catholicity; yet, in practice, there may be, especially during the necessarily confused period of study, trial and error, and actual organization. Besides, tensions between international groups and some of their local constituents are inevitable—all the more so when nationalism, age-old or newborn, arouses susceptibilities and passions. Anyone who takes a step risks stumbling and falling. These unavoidable conflicts are the price of progress.

＊

Basically, the major problems of contemporary Catholicism arise from the fact that the Church is marching ahead in a world that is itself progressing and expanding. They are caused either by the very marching of the Church or by the different pace, too slow or too fast, at which she and the world advance. In any case, they are a sign of life, since life is movement and movement reveals itself in growth and progress. The soundest optimism reminds us that some pains are growing pains; still, we must not forget that others forebode paralysis.

The problems that harassed the Church in ages past may have been as distressing as today's, but never were they as numerous, as multiform, as complex and as far-reaching as now. The old ones keep assuming different shapes; each new day spawns its own batch; and the need of solving both old and new presents further problems again.

I heard many people, including some theologians, show surprise because Pope Pius XII spoke so often and on such a variety of topics. What they really showed was their ignorance of the newness and the complexity of our era. Appreciating the power of opinion within the Church, he spoke out in order to educate Catholic opinion, to keep it from sleeping the sleep of the just before its time, to call its attention to every current problem from painless childbirth to the internal organization of Catholic Action, and to suggest ways to cope with the multitudinous tasks it faces today. During his entire pontificate, Pius XII, as the very voice of the Church, summoned a generation of Catholics to investigate the serious problems God has enjoined them to solve.

129

chapter five

The Spirituality
of
Contemporary Catholicism

If we would understand an era, we must study the saints it gave the world and God; for each era has its own spirituality and its own way of going to God, sometimes blazing fresh trails and sometimes traveling the old roads with a new outlook. The religious trend which bequeathed us *The Imitation of Christ* was called *devotio moderna,* "modern devotion"—and that, at the end of the Middle Ages. The saints always embody the spirituality of their times by carrying it to the utmost perfection.

As a case in point, let us recall the sixteenth century. The misunderstanding of the Reformation and the paganism of the Renaissance so diverted its energy that we can guess that age's potential only if we examine the saints it produced: Teresa of Avila, John of the Cross, Francis de Sales, Ignatius of Loyola, Francis Xavier and chiefly, perhaps, Thomas More.

We are too prone to think of the saints as creatures rapt in eternal bliss, beyond the reach of time; stained-glass figures or, rather, unconvincing abstractions that look as awkward in plaster as they must have been uncomfortable in the flesh. But we are mistaken: saints are men and, by that very fact, faithful to the vocation and the spirit of their times. For, according to God's plan, every age has potentialities to be realized in ways never seen before or after, a message to be transmitted to posterity, and a stone to be fitted into that heavenly Jerusalem which we creatures of time are building in eternity. Any age can choose to answer its calling or ignore it, to merit a "Well done, good and faithful servant" or be cast forth into the darkness outside. Thus we see the *Pax Romana* of Augustus preluding the world-wide diffusion of the Good News of Christ.

Saints help their epoch to answer its calling in two ways: by continuity or by contrast. By continuity, when, in sublimated form, they epitomize its possibilities. So Francis and Dominic baptized the communal movement and brought to a happy conclusion an attempted reform which had lapsed into heresy. By contrast, when they react violently against the error and vice around them. So Benedict Joseph Labre, in a hair shirt of lice, confuted the cynical and dissolute eighteenth century. In practice, continuity and contrast concur. Every saint falls in with his era, and every saint protests against it: falls in because of its vocation and protests because of its unfaithfulness. That is why Ignatius of Loyola founded an Order of humanists and taught them the kind of discipline that would save them from the individualism of the Renaissance and the Reformation.

*

In this twentieth century, what is Catholic spirituality like? What is a modern saint like, and how does he differ from his predecessors?

To answer these questions, we must sketch modern spirituality in general. The first feature we shall notice is the trend away from the extraordinary toward the ordinary, away from the exterior toward the interior.

First of all, asceticism is becoming simpler, more human and, to use a bizarre but accurate adjective, more democratic. Less and less of an endurance test, it is rejecting exaggerated Oriental views that ill agreed with Christian wisdom. It is also casting off the Jansenistic shackles of contempt for nature and the body, excessive introspection and individualism in matters of the soul. Indeed, it may be going too far in its reaction against the past—especially the recent past.

Fasting, vigils, disciplines and hair shirts, though still in use, have lost some of their prestige. Viewed apart from their sentimental context, they are perhaps more justly prized as means to an end. By reducing asceticism to holy poverty, Saint Francis of Assisi made a bonfire of cilices and disciplines; and, even if it burned but briefly then, the light of his teaching has been rekindled in our day by the new birth of Franciscan spirituality. Sparked partly by the studies of Sabbatier and Jörgensen, Franciscanism has, since the end of the nineteenth century, spread beyond strictly Franciscan groups, like the Third Order, to the whole Church, to Protestants and even unbelievers, so that today we can all feel its luminous warmth. It is being communicated to the clergy by the priests of the Prado, whose founder, Father Chevrier, deliberately linked his spirituality to the Franciscan tradition.

There is a "little way" which leads us to God if we gladly accept each day's lowly tasks and joys and sorrows. How strange to find it traveled by that giant of asceticism, Charles de Foucauld, and the "little saint" of Carmel, Thérèse of Lisieux—two beings so different as to seem almost irreconcilable, two whose deeds and writings determined the two chief trends in the spiritual life of our century. The message of Charles de Foucauld is rather more directed to the Little Brothers of Jesus and to the Fraternities now being erected all over the world. More widely broadcast, that of Saint Thérèse becomes ever deeper as it is allowed to speak for itself without the stylization and the complications imposed on it by eulogists. In point of fact, both trends reach the same goal; both messages teach the same truth. As truth is one, so are they.

More and more of our contemporaries equate asceticism with the heroic and loving performance of what moralists call the duties of one's state in life. Today, the extraordinary often lies in the perfection of the ordinary.

Like asceticism, mysticism is becoming less esoteric too. The marvelous tickles the curiosity of half-believers and sensational journalists more than it interests Catholics who clearly understand what the Faith is about. Chronologically, we are not far from the days when that remarkable Capuchin, Joseph of Cupertino, used to fly to the top of yonder tree; psychologically, however, we are further from them than from the days of the First Epistle of Saint Clement or the Epistle to Diognetus. Miracles still happen but, except for signs like the dancing sun at Fatima, the accent is on message rather than spectacle. It seems, too, that miracles in the moral order impress the modern mind more than prodigies in the physical: the conversion, life and death of persons like Charles de Foucauld, Eve Lavallière and Edith Stein, and the total abnegation of Father Damien among his lepers astonish even frivolous and selfish souls. There are stigmatics among us, of whom the best known and most discussed is Teresa Neumann; there are mystics also, with visions and revelations, unusual states and extraordinary phenomena—men like Father Lamy, the pastor of La Courneuve, whose utter simplicity inspired respect, or Padre Pio, who has had to escape from the enthusiastic curiosity of his fellow Italians. Still in all, the fundamental tendency of our times is quite different. It finds expression in the autobiography of Saint Thérèse of Lisieux; [1] in the diaries and letters of Elisabeth Leseur or of Pierre and Mireille Dupouey; in the spiritual writings of Charles de Foucauld; in the works of Marius Gonin, Eugène Duthoit, Toniolo, Contardo Ferrini and Léon Harmel; in *The True Disciple* by Father Chevrier; and in the lives of docker Matt Talbot [2] or seamstress Marguerite Sinclair. The mystics themselves give advice consonant with the doctrine of the little way. They seek God, not along steep and wondrous ways bordered by visions and dragons, but along the straight, level and nonetheless arduous path of love quietly proved in prayer and in the duties imposed on it by the times in which we live. Thus the ordinary and the extraordinary, the banal and the sublime, meet and melt into one.

By an analogous movement, spiritual discipline is turning its attention from the exterior to the

1 See *The Story of a Soul* (The Newman Press, 1957).—Tr.
2 See *Matt Talbot and His Times* by Mary Purcell (The Newman Press, 1955).—Tr.

interior, from fences and props to the will at the center of every man. After the flowering of Eastern and Western monasticism, the rules of an Order, the assistance received from a well-run community and the very convent walls were long deemed almost indispensable to holiness. Whoever achieved sanctity in the world was one of those happy and unaccountable exceptions that, occasionally, prove the rule. Saint Francis de Sales contradicted this general belief when he founded the Order of the Visitation to call upon the sick and the imprisoned; but, mighty innovator though he was, he eventually had to yield to pressure and cloister Mme. de Chantal and her spiritual daughters. It took a whole generation and the efforts of Saint Vincent de Paul for public opinion to admit that the Daughters of Charity could exist with no other enclosure than obedience.

Today, almost everyone agrees that souls with special contemplative or reparative vocations require cloisters and that persons living in the world can build their own interior Carmel there through personal discipline. Contemplative vocations are still numerous among men and women alike, and are even increasing in the United States now that that land of "get up and go" feels the need of contemplation ever more acutely. Lay vocations, if we may use the term, are also multiplying, according as the concept of *cloister* is broadened and the faithful realize that everyone can carry his cloister within himself amid the madding crowd and even into the subways of our sprawling cities. Both vocations fuse and work shoulder to shoulder when Florence's mayor, Giorgio La Pira, backs his crusade for justice with the prayers of cloistered nuns. The idea of community life among the diocesan clergy has developed in the most diverse ways; expanding Catholic Action has stimulated spirituality; the Franciscan, Dominican and Carmelite Third Orders have adapted themselves to present-day needs; lay groups and those new organisms termed "secular institutes" have grown so thick and fast that it is difficult to keep count; conversely, the Little Brothers and the Little Sisters of Jesus have been seeking new forms of the contemplative life closely related to the experience of the laity—and all this under the impulsion of the same deep-rooted tendency.

All in all, contemporary spirituality encourages holiness among laymen by showing that it is accessible to all, regardless of age, sex or state in life. Just as other concepts of sanctity have characterized other periods, so this ideal of holiness among the laity typifies our era without, however, excluding different views and possibilities.

Time was when monks dominated the scene: followers of Saint Martin or Saint Columbanus, Benedictines, Cluniacs and Cistercians. Then came the mendicant Orders—the Franciscans, the Dominicans and the Carmelites—with more freedom of movement. Freer still and more flexible were the Jesuits, founded in the sixteenth century. In the seventeenth, priests grouped into societies like Saint-Sulpice and the Oratory, the Lazarists and the Theatines. And so on down the centuries. The layman was certainly not forgotten in the course of this development—what with the several Third Orders, all patterned on that of Saint Francis—but the spirituality taught him usually leaned heavily on some religious Order and often seemed an artificial transposition of conventual life to the lay state. In the seventeenth century, the Company of the Blessed Sacrament, under high-minded men like cobbler Buch and aristocrat Renty, tried to remedy matters; for many reasons, however, their rather original enterprise was cut short. For our day was reserved the idea of a lay spirituality as proper to laymen as sacerdotal spirituality is to priests. The Third Orders still function as schools for the soul, but, over and above their legitimate divergences, there is being evolved a spirituality common to all laymen.

*

That is what I meant by the awkward yet apt expression "Holiness is becoming democratic." Sanctity is for every one of us, if only we accept it actively with all it entails. That this truth is being more generally understood is apparent from the success of hagiographers and spiritual writers like

Father Plus and Father Charles [3] just yesterday, and Thomas Merton, Dorothy Dohen and Father Voillaume today. Yet more significant is the elaboration of a specifically familial spirituality and the expansion of what we call "family groups." In France, the renewal of the family has produced *l'Association du mariage chrétien, l'Anneau d'or* and the "family groups" formed around youth movements, scouting, the Companions of Saint Francis, and the like; it has offered the uplifting example of couples like Pierre and Mireille Dupouey or Joseph and Alice Ollé-Laprune. But, far from being confined to France, this rebirth is universal, as proved by the admirable success of Cana Conferences in the United States and of the marriage courses given throughout the United States and Canada. I once discussed all this with an old man, a genuine Catholic, whose family life had attained near perfection. "My children are luckier than I," he said. "Mine has been a completely happy marriage; but if, when I married, I had known what they know now, it would have been still happier and, especially, more truly Christian." His observation condensed the spiritual riches of our age.

[3] The following books by these authors have been published by The Newman Press:

by Raoul Plus, S.J.: *Facing Life: Meditations for Young Men* (1950); *Holiness in the Church* (1950); *How to Pray Well* (1948); *Living with God* (1950); and *The Path to the Heights* (1954);

by Pierre Charles, S.J.: *Prayer for All Times* (1950).—Tr.

Because of our human limitations and our inability to see the whole truth at once, today's glorification of marriage and the family may have temporarily eclipsed the beauty of celibacy and the glory of virginity. But the shadows will pass and the light will shine again. Many young Catholics are once more beginning to grasp the role to be played in the Church by celibates, whether priests, religious or laymen. Vocations to celibacy among lay people are increasing in secular institutes—even those for men—like the Company of Saint Paul and the *Opus Dei*. Deeper understanding of conjugal and familial spirituality has enhanced the value of celibacy and virginity, so that they are now appreciated as vocations in the full sense of the word—not only negatively as a mortification or an exercise in asceticism, but more positively as a means to greater love.

*

Having viewed the growth of lay spirituality, let us now look at its basic principles. There are five. First, laymen need an interior and personal discipline. Unable, by definition, to join a religious community, they must inform their lives with the spirit of the vows of poverty, chastity and obedience—in other words, with the spirit of the Gospel —by observing a rule tailored to their individual needs, capabilities, state and manner of life. Secondly, they must sanctify themselves in and

141

through the temporal. As lay persons, they live in the world and are immediately responsible for it; they save their souls by saving it and by radiating Christ around themselves, in their family, their profession, their social milieu, their country, their civilization and all mankind. Thirdly, their holiness lies in the heroic practice of the so-called natural virtues, since justice, fortitude, prudence and temperance together with related virtues, like sincerity, loyalty, kindness, simplicity and magnanimity, present a common meeting ground for Christians and humanistic pagans. Fourthly, in their apostolic work Catholic laymen must always combine action and contemplation. An abiding sense of inadequacy and sinfulness forces activity to rely on contemplation, just as charity urges the soul to impart its lights to others. Lastly, persons in the world should practice the type of asceticism best suited to them: that rational and methodical service known as the "little way," which consists in prompt fidelity to God's will manifested in the duties of one's state in life. A simple path, it should nevertheless not be despised; for, in this age of persecution, in Hitler's Germany and now in Hungary and Red China, it has proved capable of gently leading souls to the stark heights of martyrdom.

Is this insight into the nature of the spiritual life evolution or involution, a product of modern thought or a return to primitive Christianity? As

142

worded, the question is unfair and unanswerable. Life and progress assert themselves in the increasing differentiation between various organs; consequently, there can be no question of reverting to the rich but undifferentiated days of beginnings and buds and promises. Besides, the existence of a laymen's spirituality does not suppress the diverse schools of monastic, religious or priestly spirituality; on the contrary, it presupposes them. Neither does modern spiritual doctrine feel superior to older forms, for that would be unjustifiable pride; instead, it acknowledges itself naturally and inevitably inferior to those states in life which permit fuller dedication of one's activity to God. The awakening of today's laity is, rather, like a fresh outpouring of the living waters contained in the Gospel. Like Catholic Action, it is not an absolute novelty but consists in a long, percipient look at some of the potentialities inherent in the Church since her foundation. In a way, we are always early Christians, since each generation sets out anew on the adventure that is Christianity.

Our own adventure, I believe, is that of lay holiness spread far and wide among the faithful. Sanctity, further, is becoming increasingly imperative in a materialistic world where apostasy and frightful inhumanity render the profession of Christianity more difficult and more dangerous. The persecutions of our day are intent on preserving the mere outward forms of Christianity, the better to disembody it and sever its connection with history; accordingly, they often subvert the laity before attacking the clergy. This fact contains a lesson: the time has come for Saint John's *turbam magnam,* that "great multitude" of saints "which no man can number out of all nations and tribes and peoples and tongues." Holiness is no longer a specialty whereby a few volunteers sacrifice themselves for the mediocre masses; like it or not, it is the duty of every Christian.

*

Now, a saint is a witness—a martyr, in the original sense of the word. Before a court of law, a witness testifies concerning a fact (as when he swears that something has or has not happened) or concerning morality (as when he commends or condemns someone's character or intentions). Before the judgment seat of his epoch, a saint bears witness to a fact, because his words and deeds attest the greatest event in history—the Resurrection of Christ; and to moral character, because his actions declare that Christ is living and holy in His Church. He speaks the language of his time; he answers the judges' questions—that is, he answers the needs and aspirations of his era.

We are being strangled by materialism—not only the philosophical kind but the practical materialism that motivates many Christians whose conduct and, therefore, inmost thoughts contradict their

144

outward show of religion. To lay hold of believers and drag them into the quagmire of materialistic tenets—that is now the world's supreme victory. Since the men who question him are imbued with theoretical or practical materialism, the Christian must take them as they are, appeal to the vestige or need of truth in them, and give them signs they understand.

As a result, sanctity nowadays necessitates respect for matter and the flesh, which are good in themselves like everything that comes forth from the hands of God. We must shake off the sequelae of Platonism, Manichaeanism, Cartesianism and Jansenism. We should remember that Christ took upon Himself a real body of real flesh, shed real tears and real blood, worked almost all His miracles to heal poor suffering bodies, and multiplied loaves and fishes to satisfy hungry stomachs. Let us return to the Thomistic and humanistic view of the composite that is man: in him, body and soul are neither bitterly opposed nor neutrally juxtaposed, but fashioned to collaborate fully in perfecting the person. The wisdom of this moderate view is all the more opportune now when, weakened by the pace of city life, we no longer have the robust, muscular, sanguine physiques of our ancestors—our rich ancestors, at least. Francis Thompson, the Catholic poet, has reminded us of these truths with a typically British blend of pity and humor.

Barring some exceptional vocation, today's saint will respect his body, considering it, neither cage nor sack nor rag, but his instrument, his companion here in time and, after the resurrection, in eternity. Even more will he respect the body of others, since it is the avenue that leads to their soul. He will give hygiene, sports and fresh air their rightful place in his life and even incorporate them into his asceticism. That this can be done I have proved to myself; how it can be done I have tried to outline in *Spiritualité de la route*. Among our dearest patrons now are Saint Luke, Saint Cosmas and Saint Damian, whose ideals actuated men like Doctor Laënnec and Doctor Récamier, and continue to elicit the priceless testimony of today's Catholic doctors, nurses and nursing sisters.

Respecting matter entails respecting material causes, the importance of which has been re-emphasized by Jacques Maritain. Now, respecting material causes means appreciating the role they play in history, being attentive to the material welfare of the people and ensuring the soundness of their technological and economic structures. In this socialized world of ours, we must understand that almsgiving, though it has not altered its nature, has broadened its scope. Consider the scientist who discovers an untapped source of energy, unguessed food resources in nature's cupboard or a new way to alleviate pain; the economist who devises a better system of distributing wealth among individuals or peoples and, especially, between rich nations and underdeveloped ones; or the mayor who inaugurates an effective program for solving the housing problem in his city—consider them, I say, and you will realize that they are giving alms, perhaps not more meritoriously, but certainly more effectually than those who distribute bread and money to the poor and build shelters for the homeless. If there is always need of dispensing charity immediately and directly, there is even more need of doing so indirectly, with a long-range plan and according to the multiform needs of human nature. Is that not what Adenauer and de Gasperi did when they gave back to their fellow citizens a desire to live and a minimum of well-being? Is that not what Christian employees of the Food and Agriculture Organization or of health boards do every day? The modern saint looks forward to technical advances and economic improvements because he knows that subhuman conditions, like those of proletarians or paupers reduced to begging, block the way to divine grace.

While giving matter its due, he will strive to disorient materialists by making them stumble upon manifestations of the spirit. Because our contemporaries believe only what they can see and touch, they must be made to see and touch the spiritual; because they trust only experience, they must be helped to experience freedom. Now, freedom is discernible only by its effects. That is why a saint, by the very originality of his thought and the spontaneity of his conduct, can so clearly demonstrate the existence of spirit and freedom, and so cogently invalidate the explanations of materialism and determinism. In a world where everything is calculated and foreseen, he deals in the unforeseeable; in a world where everything carries a price tag, he represents selfless giving. Always an integral part of holiness, the folly of the Cross is most meaningful now. Brother Albert gives up painting to serve the poor; "Our Lady's fool," Father Maximilian Kolbe,[4] becomes the saint of a hellish concentration camp; Hans and Annette Scholl, with no hope of success, organize the White Rose to counter Adolf Hitler. On the surface, their actions may seem fruitless, their lives wasted; but they have been eminently purposeful: proof of the freedom of the soul and the disinterestedness of love. If the risen Christ bared His wounds to Thomas' sceptical fingers, shall we do less?

*

Cheek by jowl with materialism stalks utilitarianism. *Effectiveness, efficiency,* these are the grim but magic watchwords of an era that has come to deny the existence of objective truth and morality. Today, that only is good and true which serves a particular end, the nation's welfare or the success of the revolution. We Christians must denounce

[4] See *Our Lady's Fool* by Maria Winowska (The Newman Press, 1952).—Tr.

this disastrous falsification of values by proclaiming the truth, come what may, and refusing to twist it to the shape of some short-lived cause.

At the same time, we should recall the Gospel saying that a tree is judged by its fruits. Have we not too often felt the truth to be our truth, our private property, our household god? Truth is life and therefore must unfurl, since the essence of life is growth and fruitfulness—not ephemeral and superficial success, but something deep and lasting. There is no use announcing the glad tidings of Christ if we look sad and soured; no use averring that ours is the noblest system of morality if we do not practice it; no use pretending we know the answer to every problem if we never solve any; no use insisting we hold the key to the interpretation of history if we are always one or two revolutions behind. The romanticists' acquiescence to failure is worlds removed from holy abandonment to God's providence. Let that pensive cavalier, Don Quixote, forever champion lost causes. But not Teresa of Avila, the daughter of knights: she loved to fight and was unwilling to lose. Christians espouse but one cause: God's, which includes man's salvation; and their victory is already assured.

The most active saints—men like Remy of Reims, Bernard of Clairvaux and Vincent de Paul —trained themselves to perceive the major trends

149

in history, not to follow them blindly, but to evaluate and direct them to God. That an action is beautiful in proportion as it is useless—this is a stoic, not a Christian, concept. We ought never to confuse gratuitousness and uselessness. The testimony of a saint in no way resembles André Gide's famous "gratuitous deed." No: by the only standards that count, that testimony is always supremely efficacious, just as the deepest passivity of a mystic is supremely active. Christ wrought no idle miracles; and when He died on the Cross, He did so gratuitously, not uselessly.

"Out-of-date" and "impotent"—such are the chief charges leveled at our religion today. Sanctity must, therefore, prove itself timely and effective, remembering all the while that, according to the perennial paradox of Christianity, timeliness often looks untimely and effectiveness ineffective. The Church wants men of action to build institutions, found spiritual and temporal communities, organize society, reform politics and establish social justice and peace. In short, she wants the type of apostles whom Léopold Levaux has aptly described as "structural missionaries"—men like those pioneers of the Catholic Social Movement: Ozanam, Léon Harmel, Marius Gonin, Eugène Duthoit, Giuseppe Toniolo and so many others who have achieved smaller fame or received less general approbation. (The fact that the

Church has initiated beatification proceedings for Ozanam, Harmel and Gonin is, incidentally, a sign of the times.) Of the same caliber were the priests who inspired and sustained them: among others, *abbé* Thellier de Poncheville, who was proclaimed "France's greatest priest" just as La Tour d'Auvergne was her finest soldier. So, too, were the originators of Catholic trade-unionism: Zirnheld, Maria Bardot, Madeleine Carsignol; and the early founders of Catholic Action: Fernand Tonnet, of Belgium's Young Catholic Workers, as well as "*Monsieur Paris,*" Joseph Lotte, Pierre Poyet and André Martel among university people. By establishing the Propagation of the Faith to save heathen souls with yarn winders' pennies, Pauline-Marie Jaricot did more for the missions than did hundreds of perfervid sermons. With beatification, the Church holds her up to be imitated. By "inventing" the practice of family allocations, Emile Romanet did more for the family and social justice than twenty sapient tomes on the just wage.

What I have just said does not alter the fact that the Church always needs those who, exteriorly, seem to be doing nothing; she needs the silent holocausts of the cloister, the merits of the sick in hospitals and sanitaria, the rosaries of old women whose hearts are as wracked with love as their hands are gnarled with work. She constantly looks to the followers of Thérèse of Lisieux, the apostle and missionary of Carmel and the patroness of all who can only remain silent, suffer and die. Contemplation and action are inseparable.

That term, *action*, is one of the key words of the age. Our contemporaries love action to idolatry. They even confuse it with busyness. And we Catholics are, in this respect, too typically the children of our time. So many make the apostolate an excuse for restlessness! So many mistake puttering and meddling for social work! So many trust to the infallible techniques of propaganda, forgetting that propaganda usually works best when it moves the masses from below—from the stomach up! They are not apostles and builders, but self-seeking busybodies with a mania for movement. A saint may be superhumanly active; he may draw crowds, as when Bernard of Clairvaux preached the Crusade or Paul of the Cross drove sinners to the confessional; like Vincent Ferrer, he may sometimes even be an agitator; but he is never agitated —still less, fanatical.

Amid today's din, the "moment of silence" observed at official ceremonies seems almost a heroic act. Into this atmosphere the saint must march with a column of silence. Modern man disperses his attention, imagination and memory over too wide a range of interests; he keeps snipping away at his divided will; he systematically ignores his conscience and his true nature and lets himself be

152

caught in a mad whirl of external activities. To this tendency the saint must oppose meditation, reason, concentration, a deep and intense interior life—in a word, everything that prayer makes possible, everything that makes prayer possible. Unless today's Catholics do likewise, they may be "decent fellows" and even "good Christians," as we say, but they will never attain a genuine spiritual life. We could all learn a lesson from *abbé* Monchanin, a very silent soul who was also a profound thinker and a dynamic missionary.

But the spirit of prayer, which is ever essentially the same, admits of different forms according to circumstances. Nowadays, the prayer of persons outside the cloister must be geared to action. By rendering recollection difficult and making them rashly trust in their own strength, action may turn them away from prayer; conversely, failure, discouragement and inevitable disgust can show them their inadequacy, foster a feeling of aloneness and so lead them to prayer. If activity can overshadow the presence of God, it can also make workers long for His sunshine. For modern saints, action is a handy gauge of inconsistency and incompetence; more positively, it is a goad that urges them to forsake comfort, laziness and self-love in order to make their dreams realities. Many laymen are tied up by their duties of state or tasks forced on them by necessity. Without neglecting longer and more regular converse with God, they should perhaps make their prayer consist in thinking of Him fervently throughout the day when and as circumstances permit. Thus, they will pray, discontinuously but frequently, as they meet resistance or support, taste failure or victory, feel joy or sorrow, receive humiliation or encouragement, or glimpse divine beauty in the blue of the sky or the eyes of man. So far, mystical theology has explored silence and solitude; it has yet to study the possibility of recollection amid tumultuous activity. A heartening example shines in the life of Marius Gonin, who, though busy and sick, remained rapt in God.

*

The garden of prayer is watered in two ways: by eternal springs, like the Gospel or the worship of the Church; and by temporary channels, like the spiritual writings and the devotions of a specific period. Our era is very noticeably leaving secondary sources further and further behind and drinking deep draughts from the everlasting fountainhead of all life. Our spirituality is characterized by the rediscovery of the Bible and the liturgy.

Without discarding ancient works on spirituality, we are not giving all of them the same importance they once had. How many people still read Scupoli's *The Spiritual Combat*? Even *The Imitation of Christ* and *The Introduction to a Devout Life* do not have as large a public as formerly. We prefer either Scripture itself—both the Old and the New Testaments—or the early Fathers of the Church. A hundred years ago, so few Catholics read the Bible that it seemed the dowry of the Reformation; they hardly knew the Epistles, the Acts of the Apostles or the Apocalypse; and when they read the Gospels (which was not often enough), they usually relied on synoptic versions and mediocre translations. That matters are different today is incontestably proved by the many different editions of the Bible published by Catholic houses, beginning with those two masterpieces: the *Bible de Jérusalem* and the English translation by Monsignor Knox. French Catholics are now singing scriptural texts to the melodies of Father Gelineau and his fellow workers.[5] The acclaim accorded writers like Father Chevrier stems from the fact that their spiritual teaching flows directly from the Gospels and Saint Paul. Present-day spirituality is Biblical.

It is liturgical, too. Our generation is reaping a rich harvest sown by Solesmes and Dom Guéranger in France, Beuron Abbey in Germany, and Maredsous, Lophem and Mont-César in Belgium. As was fitting, the liturgical movement began with the Benedictines and then spread to all the religious

[5] These texts and melodies have been adapted to various languages and are being sung in many countries. The following versions are available in English: *Twenty-Four Psalms and a Canticle* (Toledo, Ohio: The Gregorian Institute of America); and *Thirty Psalms and Two Canticles* (London: The Grail).— Tr.

Orders, every branch of Catholic Action, and parishes like that of *abbé* Remillieux in Lyons or of *abbé* Michonneau in Paris. Experience teaches that a parish revives when the liturgy comes to life. Here again statistics clearly picture the tendency. A genuinely liturgical missal, for instance, was once a rarity; but today, thanks to the initiative of Dom Gaspar Lefebvre, real missals are being published in an endless variety of editions and sold in huge shipments all over the world. The significant changes which Pius XII made in the liturgy of Holy Week, the easing of the Eucharistic fast and the enthusiastic reaction to evening Masses disclose the breadth and the depth of this liturgical revival. As a result of it, private devotions have yielded ground to the official prayer of the Church, evening Masses often replace holy hours or group recitation of the rosary, the Mass and the Eucharist are beginning to assume their rightful place at the center of our religious life, and the community spirit of the liturgy is gradually supplanting the individualism of bourgeois days.

Meanwhile, we sometimes exaggerate and react violently against the past. We make all sorts of mistakes: over-eager or ill-instructed, we interpret scriptural texts imprudently; in an effort to be faithful to the spirit of the liturgy, we foster dubious innovations or cling to pointless archaisms; we foment heated but futile controversies on matters like saying Mass facing the congregation; we sometimes neglect personal for collective prayer and overburden religious services with explanations and commentaries. At the same time, we encounter all forms of passive resistance, so that the progress of the Biblical and the liturgical movements varies markedly in different countries and even parishes. Slight or serious mistakes on the one hand and deliberate or unconscious inertia on the other—these are the inevitable price of improvement, and we should be unfair if we emphasized them to the point of denying or underestimating the over-all progress.

Comparing two churches—the one baroque and the other modern—will help us visualize the change that has come over religious feeling. In the baroque structure we have splendor and bombast, a fustian show of magnificence sometimes only stucco deep, a profusion of statues and paintings, and the main altar far removed from the congregation. In the modern one we find simplicity and poverty, a somewhat puristic concern for openness and austerity reflected on the bare walls, a minimum of paintings and statues, with the main altar as the focal point. The old folks murmur, "They're changing our religion," yet contemporary spirituality and prayer are but returning to the perennial source of all prayer and spirituality. Is this not providential at a time when brutal new facts and critical minds are forcing man to re-examine every aspect of life?

*

For the world is in a state of revolution. In the wake of the four horsemen of the Apocalypse, devastated lands are piled high with the ruins of charred buildings, crumbling institutions, disintegrating cultures and changing civilizations. A new order is coming into being—one which will differ radically from the old ones and, very likely, from the dreams of those who think they are shaping it.

Under the circumstances, there is no room for complacence. Any saint today must be a revolutionary. I do not mean he is bound to follow docilely every avant-garde movement; but I do mean this: he must understand that this is no time for cautious lagging and pious routine but, rather, for severance, daring, availability, service and speed. More than ever before, today's saints must be "Sons of Thunder."

Severance should be nothing new to us Christians, bound as we are by our faith to break with the world, with sin and with ourselves. Availability, without which we could never answer God's call, will help us to face the countless and often disagreeable surprises that follow social upheavals, and to judge them with that blend of good will and common sense which are the hallmark of intellectual charity. Until recently, speed has perhaps not characterized the children of light, who have almost always been outdistanced by the sons of darkness. It is, then, high time we recall that the dove, which symbolizes simplicity, flies straight from one point to another and that the serpent, which represents prudence, strikes and darts away faster than the eye can see. This revolutionary atmosphere compels us to exchange material ease and intellectual comfort for hazard and adventure. We should no more complain about it than about any other means Providence uses to make us detached and generous.

What will come of all this turmoil? Something new, naturally. But will it be really new, sounder, more human? Much as we hope so, we cannot be sure. In any case, the reappraisal of age-old ideas and social structures and the shaping of new theories and institutions have occasionally bared the workings of freedom in the evolution of history. We can easily observe that fact in our day when, after the liberal and organizational revolutions of the nineteenth and twentieth centuries, a third revolution is seeking to humanize social relations.

Modern saints must try to establish justice wherever freedom has gained a foothold. In the present crisis, charity is proved by justice, and justice by deeds. Though always metaphysical, the major errors now appear to the masses under sociological

159

aspects and pass themselves off as an ersatz not only for faith but for hope and charity. Hence, our charity must be resourceful enough to become social and to kindle hope; hence, the importance of social justice in contemporary spirituality. If *abbé* Pierre has roused so many Catholics to action, it is because they saw action was imperative—for their very salvation.

In this new world of ours, slings and arrows may pain and outrage us, but never should they vanquish us. Its very apocalyptic atmosphere should not depress us but, instead, incite us to rediscover the Apocalypse itself, which too many dismiss as incomprehensible. The glow of conflagrations heralds the second coming of Christ and should fill us, not with servile fear, but with exultation. Apocalyptic times call for apocalyptic Christians.

Among other distinctive achievements, contemporary spirituality has rediscovered the meaning of eschatology: awaiting the Saviour's Parousia, the last judgment, new heavens and a new earth; and, in so doing, it has rediscovered the meaning of history. Ensconced in their individualism, past generations of Christians considered the four last things from their own standpoint to the detriment of the world; they worried about the particular judgment but forgot the general. Their view of history and their static conception of the universe

160

obfuscated those essential and soul-nourishing truths which, uncovered anew, give us hope today.

In truth, we have infinitely more reason to hope than to despair. The present-day saint must, nevertheless, take upon himself his era's anguish—say, the sort voiced by the existentialists—and transform it. Shutting himself up in hope as in an ivory tower would be egoistic. He must comprehend the despair of the sinner who feels trapped in quicksand evil; of the unbeliever who, now that God is dead, howls like a mad dog under an empty sky; and of the stoic who clings to freedom as final proof that life is meaningless. Most young Catholics now realize that a delirious man needs, not a spoonful of syrup, but, sometimes, a red-hot iron to cauterize his flesh. That is why they reject emollient compromises, lenitive distinctions, trite solace, pious rhetoric and saccharine fancies. The Church no longer requires overgrown altar boys; she wants men-at-arms, the poor of Christ, fighters and intrepid virgins to stand in the arena and defy the jaws of lions and the folly of men. God or nothing—that is the choice before us today. Those who prefer nothing must be made to feel their nothingness, must be converted from the idols they worship and awakened from their opium dreams. To everyone we are bound to reveal God, not so much in our words (for they may sound like so much cant) as in our living. Charity enables to-

161

day's saint to plumb the depths of despair and face the pale phantom of suicide; but faith and hope allow him, like an expert diver, to touch bottom only to rise more swiftly toward the light which is God.

*

A saint first senses the despair of the forsaken and betrayed throngs when he tries to alleviate their material and spiritual misery. Whether he wills or no, his life is tied in with the masses, and he cannot abandon them to assure his own salvation or tend a little flock of chosen souls. He is responsible for the many, since God has entrusted them to him. However depersonalized it may look, each atom of humanity conceals a person who suffers silent frustration, a reservoir of freedom, a ready land which God's grace can fill with flowers. The formless multitude itself contains potential communities that will eventually ensure its human dignity.

Like the crucified Christ, who endured the sarcasm of insolent men and the spittle of fools, every saint is bound to seek humility, utter poverty, complete abjection; and that is what he will find if he loses himself "in the heart of the masses," for there he will drink the dregs of misery and know the agonizing experience of being an absolute nobody, a social security number, a welfare case or another

162

robot in the factory down the street. Such is the ultimate idea behind specialized Catholic Action since the organization of the Young Catholic Workers; such is the secret of the missionary activity so strikingly exemplified by the Little Brothers and the Little Sisters of Jesus.

Being a Christian and, consequently, a free man, no saint can shun today's dechristianized and dehumanized hordes. His freedom will be disconcerting, his purity shocking, and his justice offensive. Let him expect to be the bête noire of the mighty, who have to keep the masses sunk in spiritual misery. Let him also expect, like the prophets whom Israel stoned, to be deemed the enemy of those very people for whom he lays down his life. To differ from the crowd in nothing but holiness is a commendable aim but by no means a safe one, for it does not shield a saint from the jealous wrath of the many, especially when their passions are stirred by the double-dealers who exploit them. As man, Christ differed from the rest of humanity in sinlessness alone; still, the people of Jerusalem, after having cheered Him along His palm-strewn way, delivered Him up to Pilate to be crucified.

*

What our contemporaries find most offensive in a saint is his purity, perhaps because it fills them with a gnawing nostalgia. In this aphrodisiac civilization, sexuality dominates the realm of thought and the sexual appetite runs riot. Because of the ever-widening gap between instinct and reason, contraception facilitates love without children, and artificial insemination produces children without love. There have always been sodomites, but they used to hide for shame, whereas now they try to make their anomaly a standard for human conduct. Well before the Marquis de Sade, there were sadists, but they only half suspected their condition and failed to recognize the source of their gruesome pleasure, whereas now many sadists deliberately offer sacrifice to their interior demon. Like all knowledge of good and evil, thought begets the best and the worst: the best when it enlightens the will and keeps it from conniving with evil; the worst when it becomes the instrument of a perverse will in the service of evil. Nowadays, the worst is the rule, and the best the exception.

In his quest for peace of soul, a saint may mistake ignorance for innocence and so refuse to be enlightened. But no one has the right to ignore the truth. Whoever embraces celibacy must realize what he is giving up. Since his is the chastity of a man and not a eunuch, of an adult and not a prepubescent child, he must know with what hygienic and ascetical measures to safeguard it. He must understand that chastity is best defended by sublimation, not inhibition, and that it has being and meaning only because of charity. Whoever chooses marriage, on the other hand, should find strength in the familial spirituality which Providence has reserved for our weak generation. No longer is marriage the calling of the uncalled, but an election to the light of the Holy Spirit; no longer a cozy compromise with money and the flesh, but a summons to a glorious adventure.

The spread of Marian devotion in our day is indubitably providential. As both virgin and mother, Mary can inspire and assist consecrated celibates and married persons. She graciously adorned the house of Nazareth with silence, lowliness, self-effacement, everyday work and quiet love—the elements of a spirituality which deeply impressed Charles de Foucauld and seems especially well-suited to our time. Devotion to the Blessed Virgin may, of course, be marred by abuses like superstition, affectation, sentimentalism or—worse yet—rhetoric; but for Catholic and Protestant rigorists to see only these excesses is like concentrating on a flyspeck in the corner of a masterful painting. What really matters is that Mary is increasingly better known and better loved as the consummate exemplar of poverty and humility, the co-redemptrix of the human race and the sinless mother of sinners. That is what we were made to understand by the recent centenary of the apparitions at Lourdes, that sanctuary where the sick learn to prize bodily suffering and men from every nation are taught to love one another.

*

Christians, finally, must try to perceive in what direction the world is going. To all appearances, it has never been divided into so many hermetic and hostile fragments. Yet, modern transportation and communications are shrinking the globe and shortening the hours, as technical advances usher in a new era; and in all this activity we can see mankind searching, in the dark, for unity. Now, whatever contributes to the oneness of the human family agrees with the highest meaning of history and, even more so, with the teaching of the Gospel, since Christ's last command to the Apostles was to achieve unity in love.

When, in the fifteenth century, nations arose on the ruins of Christendom, there appeared Joan of Arc, a saint who fought for both her country and a just peace. Our era, likewise, needs saints to serve peace and the fatherland, saints who look beyond the old confines of nations and extend their charity to the world. Joan of Arc went to the stake to sanctify her country. Sanctifying the oneness of the human family will likely lead (and, indeed, has already led) today's pacific saints to those modern stakes called crematories. How many persons became martyrs for peace in nazi and communist concentration camps! If world peace and

166

unity are realized without the help of Christians, we shall have bungled our evangelical mission. The modern saint must, therefore, be an agent of peace, one of the meek who possess the earth.

The ideal of unity should illuminate our minds as we rediscover the long-neglected dogma of the Mystical Body, which, with that of the creation, establishes the brotherhood of man. That this truth so electrified the first Young Catholic Workers and Young Catholic Students tells much about the religious psychology of our day.

*

Such, then, appear to be present-day spirituality and holiness, with their riches and their appalling exigencies. When I say "present-day," I do not intend to ignore those permanent truths and conditions which the passage of time cannot alter, and especially not those virtues antiphrastically called "passive" because of the intense activity they provoke.

Saint Grignion de Monfort looked ahead to "latter-day apostles"; Monsignor Benson, in *Lord of the World,* painted "apostles of the crucified Christ." Common to both visions is the idea of holiness hidden under everyday appearances and undisclosed by any external sign. I do not know whether we are nearing the end of the world (in fact, I am hardly inclined to think so), but it seems

167

to me that contemporary holiness is patterned on de Monfort's "latter-day apostles." For that is the ideal to which present developments are leading us. Ours is a materialistic world bereft even of its idols; the sheer force of circumstances makes mediocrity unthinkable; accordingly, Christ's disciples are compelled to choose between holiness and treason. Hard words, these; but reality is harder still. Compromise and half-measures have taken flight; our bridges are burned behind us, and our ships scuttled. We have no choice but to fly into the arms of Love.

chapter six

Catholicism
and
World Needs Today[1]

What does today's world expect from the Catholic Church? Judging from appearances, nothing—and that, even in the West, which was molded by Christianity, where Catholic history is recorded at every step, where myriad crosses rise by the wayside and cathedrals always point to the heart of a city. Let missioners preach the word, let the faithful witness even unto bloodshed, let Christians build a better city, and the world answers with indifference, silence and ignorance: a leaden indifference, both ponderous and pulpy; a silence that betokens the death of thought and even curiosity; and a disenchanted ignorance which foolishly thinks itself wise and is far worse than that of pagans, since theirs is but a hungry lack of knowledge. At times, the voice of the popes, even when

---

1 This chapter reproduces almost in its entirety the address I delivered at the Second World Congress of the Lay Apostolate held in Rome in October of 1957. Despite its somewhat oratorical tone, it is included here because it seems to summarize and conclude what I have been trying to say.—J. F.

171

it announces the way to life and utters the spontaneous feelings of human nature, seems to be echoing down the empty nave of some desecrated basilica.

*

Conjure up a typical picture of the twentieth century. First you see a metropolis rearing its skyscrapers into the heavens with all the pride of Babel. Rootless, shiftless masses mill about the streets. The subways cram a crowd of individuals together who are desperately alike and just as desperately hostile. There they sit with anonymous faces that betray boredom and confusion, immured in perpetual solitude and relentlessly dragged down by the burden of everyday cares. Just what do these depersonalized mobs expect from Catholicism? Glance at the reading matter handed them by the opinion factories. The dailies tickle every type of curiosity with every type of news—every one, that is, but the Good News of Christ; the women's magazines offer millions of frustrated subscribers succedanea for love and hope. What do the writers and the readers of such material expect from Catholicism? Enter the council chambers of democracy or the anterooms of dictatorship and you will hear grave discussions on wealth and power and prestige—on everything but the essential fact that Love is not loved. What do they expect from the Catholic Church, these shepherds of nations and the flocks they are leading to the trough of plenty or the slaughterhouse of atomic war? Listen to the oracles of the day, the writers and the philosophers: some deny the existence of anything but matter, others assert that life is hell and man a futile passion; though they differ about all else, they agree that Christianity is worthless. What do they expect from the Catholic Church, they and those who drink their heady wine of error?

*

But is this the whole picture, the whole truth? Like the edelweiss blooming in the snow, certain signs point to life and interest beneath this pall of inertia. Beyond the black marble dome spread over the world, we seem to make out the first glimmer of dawn. One of the most perspicacious French sociologists, an agnostic and a Jew, featured several sentences from Pius XII in the front matter of a recent work. Simple enough in itself, his deed is significant because it is not isolated: it expresses the hope and the expectancy of others. Through the misery and suffering, the crucial and seemingly insoluble problems of the times, Jews, Protestants, Moslems, indifferentists, sceptics and militant atheists have been brought to seek, not our dim lights, but the luminous truth of the Church reflected in us. Many Catholics through-out the world can corroborate that fact from their own experience. Religious programs on radio and television draw a wide audience, as do motion

173

pictures on Christian themes. Even abstruse spiritual books captivate countless readers, and Catholic editions of the Bible rank as best sellers. When Father Lombardi speaks, Italy flocks to hear him; when *abbé* Pierre preaches a crusade of charity, France opens her heart and her purse. America interrupts her feverish activity to hear Thomas Merton discourse on the contemplative life. Scandinavia, possibly the most dechristianized part of Europe, produces Johannes Jörgensen and Sigrid Undset. At the call of Canon Cardijn, the world sends thousands of young workers to a Roman congress. Sometimes the very practices which appear superstitious to enlightened Catholics reveal a spark of smoldering faith. The callousness of the masses cannot still the anxious questioning of the human heart.

*

The antitheses between both panels of our diptych stem not only from the illogicalness and the complexity of man but also from the inner contradictions of a stormy period in which dreams, illusions, frustration, fear and hatred clash with the roar of thunder.

Man is the lord of nature like never before. He can release and control the power dormant in every atom; he has conquered time and space. With his test tubes he feels ready to re-create life; with his depth psychology he believes he can re-

174

make souls. No wonder he nurtures Promethean dreams for tomorrow. Soon, he imagines, he will cruise through interplanetary space and hop from one star to the next, make the earth infinitely productive, and fashion the bodies and souls of new human races which may someday give birth to the superman. Imagination knows no bounds, and the sky is no longer the limit. In the fully rational universe of tomorrow, everyone will have a right to a place in the sun, to happiness and bread, peace and freedom. But what would grace mean to such a complete and perfect race? And what about God?

Science fiction, the latest avatar of mythology, evokes and overcolors these wild dreams; and yet novels about the brave new world, if their authors possess any critical sense, carry undertones of irony and secret apprehension. In truth, at the very moment when man's discoveries have broadened his possibilities unto impossibility and magnified his dreams unto megalomania, a savage winter wind has pitilessly overturned the idols he fashioned with his own hands after Nietzschean prophets had announced that God was dead. And now the twilight of the idols is settling over the earth. The blast is sweeping on, like so many dead leaves, the myths on which Western thought has thrived since the Enlightenment. During the last century, the Church had to denounce the extravagant ambition of those myths; paradoxically, she must now up-

hold the element of truth they contained and safeguard it from the nihilism of our disillusioned
contemporaries. The irony of the situation, however, is only apparent.

*

Consider the myths that have grown up around
science. Though its findings, methods and spirit
are now applied to every branch of knowledge,
that very science which promised to redeem man
can tell him nothing definitive about the nature
or the meaning of his life. The progress myth
maintains that in one century mankind has gained
more wealth, power and technical know-how than
in all of previous history. Perhaps so, but our
progress has assumed the equivocal and ominous
shape of the mushroom cloud that rose over Hiroshima the first time atomic energy was used.
Hypnotized by the myth of liberalism, the masses
invoke freedom and, in its name, march right into
totalitarian slavery. The democratic myth leads
many nations to adopt the externals of parliamentary democracy. Even where it is more than an
empty mold and functions fairly well, people soon
see that, far from being a magic formula, democracy is just another political technique. Then there
is the myth of nationalism, whose strong wine always inebriates the rabble and heartens it to kill
or be killed. But older nations, stripped of sover-
eignty by international solidarity, wonder about
their future; and younger nations which have but

recently won independence, having tasted nationalism, find it bitter and notice that it solves none of
their internal problems. As for the pacifist myth,
God knows how much we talk of peace and how
shrewdly statesmen use the word as a propaganda
tool, yet never in history has the human race been
so close to a war which could annihilate it. For
fifty years now, the socialist myth has been growing
from a dream into a reality. Still, the more real it
becomes, the less fascination it holds. In its most
complete form, it resembles tyranny: capable of
rapidly setting up a cumbersome machine at
maximum cost to humanity, it is incapable of ful-
filling its deceitful promises. In its milder forms,
it soon appears inadequate and, having exhausted
its bag of tricks, can offer nothing new. Or take
the myth of revolution. Many still look forward
to a glorious revolution, but their enthusiasm
seems more a matter of habit than of conviction.
We have learned that revolutions, even when justified, do not create new men and new worlds; yet,
even now, after the liberal and the socialist revolutions, a third is breaking out to the trumpet-call
of names like Budapest, Warsaw and Bandung.
Lastly comes the myth of happiness. At the beginning of the French Revolution, Saint-Just declared, "Happiness is a new concept in Europe."
Born there perhaps, the idea is fast traveling
around the world. But everywhere it proves a will-
o'-the-wisp. Experience shows that happiness is not
a mass-produced, ready-made garment to be bought

177

in every store. We have learned that the Welfare State, though it can promote the material and collective conditions required for comfort, cannot produce happiness, that masterpiece which results from the freedom of individuals and families. If Corneille's Polyeucte returned today, he would not have to bother destroying the idols: worm-eaten, they crumble by themselves under the weight of the years.

*

When gods totter and myths explode, despair may pervade humanity and vent itself in some form of philosophical and literary existentialism. Indicative of that despair is the youth problem now plaguing the whole world—even (and perhaps especially) rich, comfort-loving nations. Millions of teen-agers gyrate in the convulsive *danse macabre* of rock 'n' roll; in Scandinavia, leather-jacketed youths flare up, smash street lights and battle the police; twenty-four thousand New York policemen try unsuccessfully to check smooth-cheeked rowdies and their gang wars; the steady increase in crimes by adolescents has England aghast; bands of restless youngsters clutter the sidewalks in the shadow of Paris' venerable Saint-Germain-des-Prés; and Russia, which once boasted of having eradicated juvenile delinquency, now faces the double problem of the young rich and the common *houliganstvo*. Such abundant, such widespread and significant facts point to only one conclusion:

178

civilization is in the throes of a crisis. With typical candor and recklessness the young reveal what adults try to hide.

Once he had stolen fire from heaven, Prometheus learned that flame was no fable but a burning, consuming reality that carried in itself the vengeance of the outraged gods. Myths are losing their currency just as money is losing its value in the spiral of inflation. Now is the time for clear, cool reason. Now, too, is the time for faith, since faith is no more opposed to reason than grace is to nature but, rather, completes reason, sustains it and orients it toward eternal wisdom. The idols are falling into dust as we brush past them. Now is the time for the naked truth, for all or nothing, double or quits. Now is the time for the Church to act.

*

Long ago, the world was in turmoil like now. The person emerged from the collectivity and saw the need of salvation. The establishment of vast empires, each with its own culture, called for universal religions. With joyful anxiety mankind awaited the Christian message of liberation. And then Christ was born. In our day, rapid, radical, global changes make the past archaic and archeological within a generation or two. Sudden transformations, as well as qualitative and quantitative shifts within the family of man, reveal unsuspected

179

dimensions and seem to plunge it into fundamentally new situations. In and through all this, the world awaits the radiant presence of Catholicism.

What, then, does the world expect from the Church and from each of us insofar as we personify her in the minds of our neighbors? First of all, I should imagine, it wants us to testify unequivocally to the immutability of divine truth and to God, who is subsistent truth. This the Carthusian monks do with thunderous eloquence in the silence of their desert; this every Catholic must do, according to his gifts and his vocation, simply because the splendor of a jealous God has forever weaned him from idols.

What is idolatry, after all, but the adoration of something relative which has been hypostatized and divinized? Little does it matter whether the idol be gold or wood, a concept or a word: there is only a difference of degree, not of nature, between kowtowing to a fetish and worshiping an abstraction; and, in truth, ideas sometimes drink more blood than Moloch himself. Ever since the coming of rationalism and naturalism, regardless of whether they developed into idealism or materialism, the human mind has been operating in a dense fog of relativity, in which outlines are blurred, objects melt into one another and coalesce or disappear, and all sense of order and perspective is lost. Guided solely by his own flickering lights, modern man is like a traveler lost on an ice-carved massif and surrounded by thousands of buttes and small lakes: with no natural landmarks and no way of getting back on the road, he must starve and freeze to death. Since man never wholly loses his sense of the sacred or his need of the absolute, he is irresistibly driven to divinize one of these relative realities; but his idol soon shows itself a mirage in the desert, an *ignis fatuus* over a marsh, dissolves and leaves him a prey to loneliness and fear.

Let us reaffirm absoluteness and transcendency, and our words, like the light from a projector, will pierce through the darkness of relativity. They will strengthen the weak and the wavering. Speaking to the rational core of man, they will present the whole question of knowledge squarely, thus: "God's creative intellect makes nature intelligible to the human mind, which was created to His image and likeness. Unless we take the truths which we apprehend by reason and refer them to the absolute, eternal and subsistent truth, they will remain partial and provisional, subject to the ebb and flow of an endless dialectic and robbed of the value they would acquire from being related to that immutable truth." Our words—and especially our deeds—will pose the problem of morality this way: "Unless referred to an absolute law identifiable with God, a person's acts cannot be right or true. His every moral decision is dictated by prejudice, passion or self-love and is stupidly gratuitous or sordidly utilitarian. So life becomes a rat race in which he works to eat and eats to work, and begets children to run the same unending circuit; so society becomes a faithless, lawless cutthroat or a colossal swindle that exacts the soul of this generation as a down payment on some gloriously happy tomorrow that is forever being postponed." We must testify to the absolute because, like nothing else, it assures consistency and solidity, uprightness and efficacy to the human acts produced by our moral conscience; it gives meaning to life—even to the most obscure and unsuccessful—by forcing us to raise our eyes to heaven and so escape the determinism of relativeness, and guaranteeing that not one tear or bead of sweat will be lost in eternity; it establishes between nations both mutual trust (that is, loyalty to agreements) and law (that is, a juridical order accepted by all for the purpose of happy co-existence); it affords stability and security in social dealings; it guards citizens against the tyranny of rulers, and rulers against the anarchy of citizens; and, finally, it can root earthly cities in justice and sow peace between them. The absolute stands security for the relative, and the unchanging and undying for what changes and dies away.

Consequently, we perceive how well the Catholic Church satisfies one of the basic aspirations of our day: the protection and the development of the human person. As proof of that ambition, we can measure the growth of the "human relations movement." Sparked by fairly pragmatic ideas on industrial relations between employers and employees and public relations between retailers and their customers, this movement has been led, by an inherent logic, to examine all the relations that exist between men in a depersonalized society which is rather more collective than communal. Behind these investigations lie the needs and griefs of all the world. When a recently decolonialized country boils over in its eager search for independence, we should look beneath nationalistic ideologies and find a deeper explanation: men's legitimate desire to be treated like adults. But we cannot protect and develop the person unless we know exactly what he is, and that we cannot know unless we refer him to the absolute; otherwise, our appreciation of him will ceaselessly oscillate between zero and infinity—the zero of crushing collectivism and the infinity of anarchic individualism. By clothing him in its own sunlight, the absolute adorns the person with that eminent dignity Leo XIII spoke of; it subjects the human person to the duties and the scale of values on which his perfection hinges, since he is contingent and dependent in his filial relation to the divine absolute.

Let us, therefore, witness to the absolute. Now that the world is awaiting our testimony, we have no time to dillydally with outgrown idols and crepuscular myths. We must courageously and uncompromisingly refuse homage to any false god. We need enough prudence and intellectual charity to discern the relative truths latent in every specious absolute. In fact, the better we appreciate their relativity, the louder we can proclaim the partial truths which our age has brought to light. Similarly, the more we look to eternity, the more we shall belong to our time; for the choice between the actual and the eternal rests on a false alternative. If the world persecutes us for not revering its ephemeral deities, it would despise us even more—and rightly so—for renouncing the absolute.

*

What else does modern man expect from the Church and from us, her children? He expects us to transmit Christ's message to him, whole and unadulterated; he wants us to tell or remind him of the living water for which he unconsciously thirsts.

He desires freedom but confuses it with license and unbridled instinct, so that, after a wild fling and a moment of lawlessness, he either falls into another form of slavery or must be more forcibly repressed than before in the interest of life in society. A few choice and master spirits achieve intellectual freedom. Unfortunately, they too often see it as a perpetual search, an open mind that will not grasp its object, or an infinite series of opinions and arbitrary choices. In any case, instinct takes its revenge. Still, this longing to be free ennobles man since it can spring only from his likeness to God. Christianity teaches us the secret of freedom: that it cannot exist without redemption, that it is not handed on like an heirloom but ever reconquered by the sword, and that it cannot be won unless grace grafts a measure of God's freedom onto our freedom of choice. Faith also reminds us that freedom, which is primarily interior and spiritual, snatches us from the servitude of sin and the tyranny of Satan, rids us of the triple concupiscence, and grows as we subject flesh and instinct to reason and reason to the truth called God. That is the profound meaning of freedom; short of it, the external liberty we cherish is an illusion. To the nineteenth century, which drank too deeply of intoxicating liberal ideologies, Catholicism seemed an authoritarian religion opposed to individual and group freedom. To our collective, organizational, committee-ridden and even totalitarian society, where anyone who wants more power is like a drunkard asking for more wine, Catholicism, which resists pressure from the masses and from governments, appears as the champion of human liberty and of those particular freedoms which further that of the spirit. The Church has not altered her teaching: tirelessly she reiterates the nature, conditions and price of freedom.

185

In its pursuit of liberty, our age is seeking a new humanism. In its wish to help the individual and the race to realize their potentialities harmoniously, it is searching for a concept and a way of life geared to present-day structures and suited to collective institutions, customs and representation. But most of our contemporaries entertain a false idea of man which leads them into one of two impasses: either they turn to the past, adopt the inadequate and oversystematic notions of liberal times, and reduce their humanism to a kind of vapid nostalgia; or they break with the past, plunge into the unknown and aspire to re-create everything from nothing, and so construct a foundationless and unbalanced humanism which can only come crashing down about them. That is why some of the most daring of modern thinkers so bitterly denounce not only the disappointing results but the very idea of humanism, and try to dull their despair in stoic indifference and resignation to failure. Their revolt against humanism is mirrored, perhaps unconsciously but no less clearly, in the distortion and the ravages inflicted on the face of man by certain schools of modern art. Even some Christians sympathize with antihumanism in their own way. Desirous of the purely spiritual and the sheerly supernatural, they spurn a tradition which runs from Clement of Alexandria, through Thomism and Franciscanism, Thomas More, Francis de Sales and devout humanism, down to Jacques Maritain—a noble tradition that asserts

186

the beauty of the Son of man and of all His brethren; the brotherhood that binds humanity and the whole of creation; the ontological and historical ascent of nature toward mankind and, through the Incarnation, of redeemed mankind toward God; and the indissoluble link between the Cross and the Resurrection, the gloom and tears of Good Friday and the radiant joy of Easter. Ours it is to guide man back to the road of true humanism, to point out that his path lies between the Mount of the Beatitudes and Mount Calvary and ends, not on earth, but in the stars. Ours to explain that humanism mutilates us if it ignores God and grace for self-reliance, and condemns us to a world of sterile suffering if it shuts out pain and hope. Just as freedom supposes that we practice abnegation and detachment, so does true humanism require us to die to ourselves and be reborn through resurrection with Christ, the Son of man.

The integral humanism we advocate embraces the whole man, body and soul, nature and grace, and can therefore deepen the meaning of current expressions which summarize some of the hopes and achievements of our age.

For the past two hundred years, for example, the West has been developing what some have called a "civilization of labor." In practice, it often seems a bitter hoax. But within the framework of Christian humanism, work is exalted to the skies and beyond, because the workman collaborates in the creative activity of the Father as well as in the redemptive mission of the Son and gives the world back to God after having completed it.

Another case in point is the "civilization of leisure" being readied by motorization, mechanization, automation and undreamed-of sources of energy. Undirected, leisure could turn to indolence; from being a slave to work, one could become a slave to bagatelles. But, inspired by Christian humanism, leisure could rise to the dignity of contemplation.

Or take the powerful and persistent movement known as feminism. Outside of Christian humanism, the emancipation of woman tends to be a fraudulent abstraction. It robs woman of her femininity and so impoverishes the human race, which can develop only through the complementary co-operation of the sexes; and it frustrates and revolts her to find herself cheated of her proper fulfillment, duped, scoffed at, and treated like a sexual object or a work horse. According to Christian humanism, the advancement of woman is effected in the midst of families founded on mutual respect—families in which the spouses, imitating the household at Nazareth, lovingly conform to the functional hierarchy inherent in

188

familial society and thereby experience their fundamental equality as persons and the differences that enable them to complete one another.

In this regard, furthermore, Catholicism does a service to womankind, the family and our epoch by extolling chastity even unto virginity. Because of scientific and medical discoveries, our generation faces a population problem such as has not yet been known. Never again can procreation be a matter of mere instinct and custom: the birth rate must be regulated and instinct ruled by reason. Artificial birth control offers no help but is tantamount to legal and generalized prostitution; for, instead of mastering instinct by reason, it subjects reason to instinct and establishes a thralldom which is all the more tyrannical since individuals and couples no longer fear the natural consequences of their actions. The one genuinely human form of birth control is self-control. Yet, the aberrations of this commercial, publicity-run, individualist and erotic civilization make us wonder whether man will ever gain mastery over his instincts. So like Sodom and Gomorrah is our world that it must be calling down the fire of heaven. By opposing this disordered civilization and rejecting artificial birth control, by proposing chastity in every state in life and glorifying consecrated virginity, the Church is rendering the human race, Homo sapiens, one of the greatest services possible today. Reason makes man the lord of creation; and, in telling him so, the Church is once again the exponent of true humanism.

*

The blood which vivifies Christian humanism is that which flowed from Christ's wounds into the veins of the Church. Its name is charity. Here is another reason why the modern world needs the Church: our age is suffering from a frightful lack of love, and charity is love carried to the highest degree. As Georges Bernanos wrote, "Now is the time when the wrath of imbeciles is boiling over." This is the hour of hatred and scorn. Class against class, trade against trade, party against party, nation against nation and race against race, all men war against one another with insults on their lips, weapons in their hands and hate in their hearts. They despise each other the more fiercely because they are growing ever more alike, separated only by material interests and aggressive instincts masquerading as ideologies. Though we may be massed together, merciless competition splits individuals and families. If these words read like pessimistic exaggeration, we need but recall the hecatombs of both World Wars, the butchery of the bolshevik revolution, the millions of Jews exterminated in Hitler's crematories, the atomic bomb dropped on Hiroshima, the bloody repression of the uprising in Hungary, and many other cases of inhumanity which we must omit, so long a task would it be to catalog the museum of contemporary horrors.

And still, the need for love is anchored deep in the heart of man—of every man, who wants to be loved individually and by name, as Christ has loved each of us. What we can and must give all men is a love that neither expects nor accepts anything in return, a love that nothing can kill or even dishearten, a love that never flags but finds infinite reason to forgive, a love like that of Vincent de Paul, Don Bosco, John of God, an insane love like that of Christ on the Cross.

To be loved in and for themselves—that is what our contemporaries desire and what our age is not doing for them. The twentieth century, we must admit, has been striving to ensure social justice. Along with the rest, Catholics have been doing their part, some belatedly and others in the forefront, mindful of the exhortations of the popes and the social teaching of the Church; in truth, we cannot overlook what every nation owes to the pioneers in Catholic social thought. At this very moment, the cause of justice is being furthered; and we as Catholics are duty-bound to promote and direct it, since our charity is but a caricature unless it impels us to fight for justice. But the results we obtain always fall short of our goal because of our limitations, human weakness and historical contingency. The institutions designed to advance social justice too often seem, not heartless, but at least impersonal, especially since our contemporaries think almost wholly in terms of commutative justice. In modern hospitals, for instance, the patients enjoy adequate care, comfort and hygienic conditions, but are they always treated like persons? And yet being treated like persons would speed their recovery as much as the costliest antibiotics. Many insurance companies guarantee salaried men a minimum of security and lift the lower classes out of misery; but when the insured stand at the cashier's window, how many are made to feel like more than a policy number? I have already mentioned the "human relations movement," which stresses that nothing can replace person-to-person dealings. Human relations of this quality, however, cannot be effected without charity, for it alone can crush the carapace of indifference, hostility or arrogance in which egoism encases each individual. The times clamor for an ingenious, imaginative, tenacious type of charity that will complete what is imperfect, fill up what is lacking and revitalize whatever institutions might sink into torpor and paralysis.

Even while serving the individual, charity must look beyond him to the edge of the continent and, farther still, to the whole world. As said before, our day has achieved some measure of social justice, but always within areas that were already rich and industrially well-equipped. Yet, more than half the world is still made up of what economists call underdeveloped countries; more than half the earth's population is still suffering from undernourishment and malnutrition—or, in plain English, from hunger. The critical problems now confronting social justice arise not so much within industrialized nations as between nations that have reached different stages of development. Far from improving, the situation tends to worsen, since the prosperous countries keep doubling their wealth and overpopulation triples the woes of the others. Fraught with grave danger, the predicament could touch off a new global conflict that would restore equality—the equality of annihilation.

His Holiness Pius XII frequently suggested that affluent groups distribute their superabundance to allow the less well-endowed to get on their feet industrially and agriculturally. Simple in theory, his solution is hard to apply, because the giants of industry are inclined to hoard their happiness jealously and display such luxury and waste as to mock the wretchedness of others. This is where collective and international charity appears necessary and becomes one with the evangelical spirit of poverty preached by Francis of Assisi. Compelled by facts and experience, economic theorists are gradually discarding pernicious old concepts like the atomistic economy of gain and competition advocated by liberal capitalism or the massive economy of power which produced monopolistic capitalism, economic imperialism and soviet socialism. They are beginning to discover an economy based on need and even on giving. And they may eventually fashion an economy of holy poverty, an evangelical economy in which wealth is for man and not man for wealth; in which everyone, individuals and groups, will divest himself of superfluities so that all may have the necessities of life, the minimum of well-being and security indispensable to the life of the spirit. The Gospel shows us the way, and the Church shows us the Gospel.

*

Once again, what does the world expect from the Catholic Church? It expects her to be catholic —that is, universal—and expects her catholicity to be reflected in the thoughts and deeds of all her children. A critic once wrote of a Catholic French author, "He is Catholic in the precise sense in which *Catholic* is opposed to *universal*." Whether the stricture was justified I do not know; but I do know that, especially now, we should not expose ourselves to such a taunt.

We are living in the age of catholicity. Urged on by dizzying progress in transportation and communications and by economic and cultural interdependence, the world is seeking unity amid strife

194

and conflict, blood and tears. We may unite and confederate, but we are not one—certainly not in mind and heart. At any moment, an infernal war could overthrow everything and halt the human caravan for centuries. Unification of the world presupposes universality of minds; and this the Catholic Church alone can foster because she is independent of nations and races and civilizations, and because by nature and in fact she is universal in space and in time. Without condemning any of the original traits which characterize peoples and civilizations, she transcends and unites them. Catholicism is the religion of an age dedicated to the universal.

A unified world will need a new culture, one that will be universally shared and will gather the attainments of all previous cultures into a living synthesis. One of the most insidious dangers ambushing today's world is the hasty extension of a spurious culture of the West which would stamp out indigenous cultures, replace them with formulae and superficial knowledge, and display the trappings of Western culture without transmitting the spirit that made it possible. Diffusing such a pseudo-civilization would multiply the number of the intellectually rootless and dispossessed. The new culture we must help shape calls for a keen sense of the new and the old, a deep understanding of tradition and traditions as well as the ability to distinguish between pure contingency and the

acquisitions which constitute the common patri-
mony of mankind. Once again the task calls for a
spirit of universality. What surer mentor could
we find than the Church? Catholic and universal,
she is implanted everywhere; she respects every
form of local culture; and her broad experience
has enabled her to integrate the treasures of
Hellenic, Latin and Oriental civilizations with the
discoveries of modern thinkers. Of course, the
Church is not a ministry of culture: her mission
lifts her far above such temporal interests. Nevertheless, all culture rests on a view of humanity, an
interpretation of life, a body of wisdom; and that
is what the Church can give us, while leaving
scholars, artists and writers free to implement it
with the materials and tools of their time, with
their own genius and that of the communities
which contributed to their development.

The Church's universality can, in addition, help
mend the rifts within contemporary society, torn
as it is by internal strife. The citizens of industrialized nations are heading toward relative social
equality, so much so that tomorrow's world may
be an aggregation of middle classes, such as is already forming in the United States. Meanwhile,
however, social conflicts keep raging, and class
struggles seem to gather ideological and emotional
momentum in proportion as the boundaries between classes are obliterated. In some countries,
where they were long treated like social inferiors,

the laboring classes have banded into a sort of workers' nation that constitutes an alien group within their own fatherland. Other categories, having lost some of their exclusive economic advantages, cling desperately to the social prestige which is now their only distinction. As a result, one sometimes feels that the men of today are separated by class confines at least as much as by national boundaries.

International differences and social antagonism could tear Christendom asunder. But the fact is that Catholicism transcends human limitations; and, by making men pray side by side in church and letting them share the same faith, the same sacraments, the same worship and the same works of charity, it can teach them the meaning of social universalism. The various labor movements, one of the most distinctive features of our era, have come of age. Now that they have had their first taste of success and responsibility, the Church can orient them toward universality and prepare the other classes and milieux for the sacrifices required by social justice.

To a world which, for the first time in history, is laying the foundations for oneness, Catholicism offers the ideal and the experience of universality.

*

All this, then, the modern world expects from the Catholic Church—and from us, too, in the very

197

name of the religion we profess. The form and pressure of the time summons us to live our faith to the full. We must not compromise or adopt half-measures. We need not travel to foreign lands in search of martyrdom: executioners make house calls nowadays and knock at our door before dawn. We cannot affect the elegant eclecticism of past ages whereby each man molded himself a religion according to his own image and likeness. The eyes of the world are upon us and force us to be what we are.

Need we remind ourselves that the Church will often be judged according to the picture we draw of her? After all, how many of our fellow men come into direct contact with the hierarchy? Or how many get to know a priest well enough to evaluate the Church by what they see in him? On the other hand, hardly a day passes without their meeting a Catholic layman, be he relative, friend or neighbor, teammate, fellow worker or townsman. Let us weigh our responsibilities: they are as heavy as the great expectations of which we have no right to disappoint the world.

The Church shall not be deaf to the cry of mankind. Her laymen shall march behind the popes and the bishops, close to their pastors and religious. Conscious of their historical responsibilities before God and men, they shall be witnesses to the divine absolute, Christians unto the folly of the Cross and Catholics in the most universal sense of the word. With each in the capacity determined by his gifts, his leanings and his vocation, they shall form but one body and one soul, like the community in Jerusalem. As the Chosen People of God, they shall dispel the anguish of the modern world and bear testimony to the truth that makes men free and the love that makes them divine.

Index

A NOTE ON THE TYPE

IN WHICH THIS BOOK IS SET

This book is set in Baskerville, a Linotype face, created from the original types used by John Baskerville, the eighteenth-century typefounder and printer. This type has long been considered one of the finest book types ever developed. The letters are wide and open and have a businesslike approach. The finer hairlines give exquisite delicacy. The heavier strokes give color and strength. The relation of the two in combination gives a brilliant effect and makes for easy reading. The book was composed and printed by the Wickersham Printing Company of Lancaster, Pa., and bound by Moore and Company of Baltimore. The typography and design are by Howard N. King.